Mission Praise Supplement

Compiled by

Peter Horrobin and Greg Leavers

MUSIC EDITION

Marshall Pickering

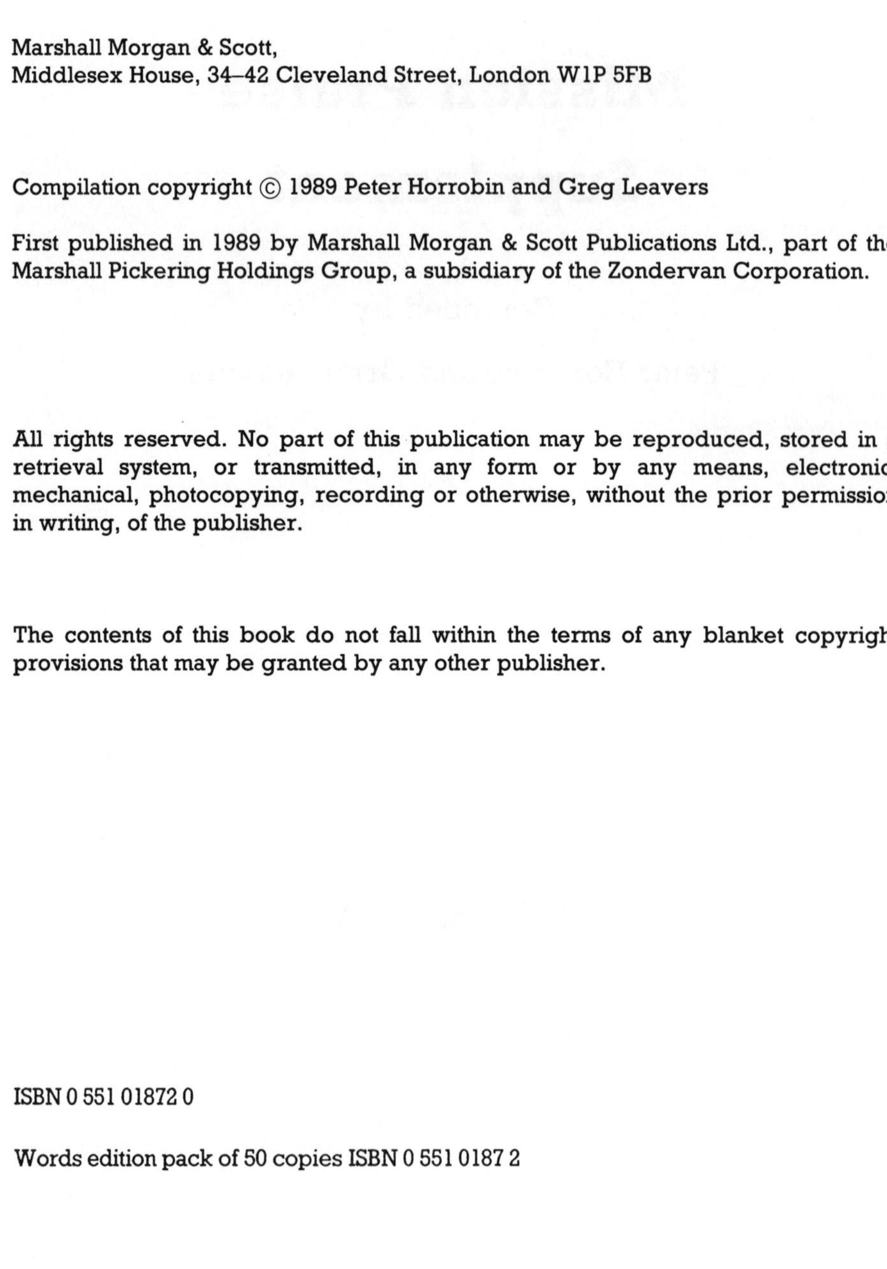

Marshall Morgan & Scott,
Middlesex House, 34–42 Cleveland Street, London W1P 5FB

First published in 1989 by Marshall Morgan & Scott Publications Ltd., part of the Marshall Pickering Holdings Group, a subsidiary of the Zondervan Corporation.

ISBN 0 551 01872 0

Words edition pack of 50 copies ISBN 0 551 0187 2

Music and text set by Barnes Music Engraving Ltd., East Sussex, England
Printed in Great Britain at The Bath Press, Avon

Foreword

This is the final collection of hymns and songs to be added to the Mission Praise stable before the production of a comprehensively indexed combined edition embracing Volumes I, II and this Supplement.

Already Mission Praise is well established as a major book for praise and worship for thousands of churches in Great Britain and, indeed, across the world. This further selection ensures that there is an adequate range of both new and older material to be used throughout the church's year and at all personal or family occasions in the Christian life. Additionally there is a rich selection of newer praise and worship songs which have the hallmark of being of lasting significance.

We trust as with the earlier volumes this Supplement will further enhance the role of music in worship as a key means of bringing individuals into a dynamic and closer relationship with the living God.

Peter Horrobin and Greg Leavers
September 1989

648 All hail the Lamb

Words and music
Dave Bilbrough

Powerfully

G Gsus G Gsus G Gsus G *Fine*

Lord.)

C/D D7 G Gsus G C/D D7

All hail the Lamb en-throned on

G Gsus G C/D D7 G Gsus

high, His praise shall be

G Am G D D7/C

our__ bat - tle cry.

D/B
G
D7/A
G
He reigns vic - to - ri - ous, for ev - er
Em
Em7
Am
glo - ri - ous, His Name is Je - sus,
to finish D.C. al Fine
to continue
D.𝄋
D
C/D
D7
G
Gsus
G
He is the Lord.

All hail the Lamb enthroned on high,
His praise shall be our battle cry.
He reigns victorious, for ever glorious,
His Name is Jesus, He is the Lord.

649 All heaven declares

Music: Noel Richards
Words: Tricia Richards

With majesty
Capo 1(A)
B♭ (A) E♭ (D) F (E) E♭/B♭ (D/A) B♭ (A)
All heaven de-clares The glo-ry of the ris - en Lord,
E♭ (D) F (E) E♭/B♭ (D/A) B♭ (A)
v.2.
Who can com-pare, With the beau-ty of the Lord?
E♭ (D) F (E)
For ev - er He will be, The Lamb up-on_ the
B♭ (A) F/A (E/G♯) Gm (F♯m) E♭ (D)
throne. I glad-ly bow the knee,

1.
2.
F7
(E7)
B♭
(A)
B♭sus
(Asus)
B♭
(A)
B♭sus
(Asus)
B♭9
(A9)
And wor-ship Him a-lone.

1 All heaven declares
The glory of the risen Lord,
Who can compare,
With the beauty of the Lord?
For ever He will be,
The Lamb upon the throne.
I gladly bow the knee,
And worship Him alone.

2 I will proclaim,
The glory of the risen Lord.
Who once was slain,
To reconcile man to God.
For ever You will be,
The Lamb upon the throne,
I gladly bow the knee,
And worship You alone.

650 Almighty God, our heavenly Father

Words and music
Chris Rolinson

With feeling

Dm
3
Al-migh-ty God, our hea-ven-ly Fa-ther, We have

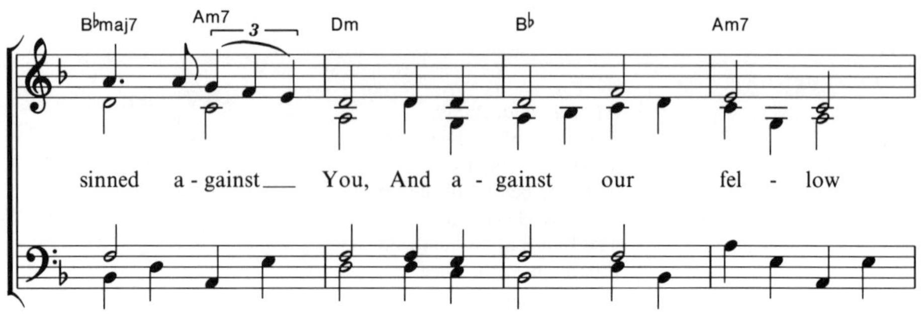
B♭maj7
Am7
3
Dm
B♭
Am7
sinned a-gainst__ You, And a-gainst our fel-low

Dsus
Dm
3
men.__ In thought and word and deed, Through

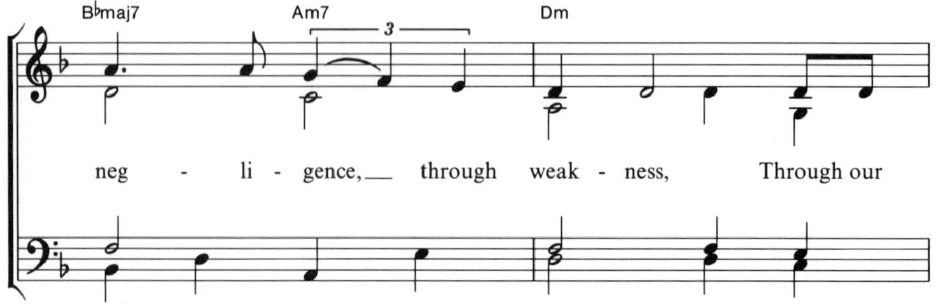
B♭maj7
Am7
3
Dm
neg-li-gence,__ through weak-ness, Through our

B♭
Am7
Dsus
own de - lib - erate fault. We are
Am
Gm7
B♭
C
F
tru - ly sor - ry And re - pent of all our sins. For the
Dm
Am7
Dsus
sake of Your Son Je - sus Christ,
Gm
B♭
C
Who died for us, who
F
B♭
G7
Am
died for us, who died for

Dsus
Dm
us,
For - give us all that is past; And
B♭maj7
Am7
Dm
B♭
grant that we may serve You In new -
Am7
D
- ness of life.
MEN: To the
Em7
A
D
Bm
Em7
A
glo - ry of Your Name,
WOMEN: To the glo - ry of Your
D
Bm
Em7
A
D
Bm
Name,
MEN: To the glo - ry of Your Name,
WOMEN: To the

rall.
Em7
A
Bm
G
D/F♯
glo - ry of Your Name, ALL: To the glo - ry of Your
Em
G
G/A
A
Dsus
D
Name. A - men, A - men.

Almighty God, our heavenly Father,
We have sinned against You,
And against our fellow men.
In thought and word and deed,
Through negligence, through weakness,
Through our own deliberate fault.
We are truly sorry
And repent of all our sins.
For the sake of Your Son Jesus Christ,
Who died for us, who died for us, who died for us,
Forgive us all that is past;
And grant that we may serve You
In newness of life.
MEN
To the glory of Your Name,
WOMEN
To the glory of Your Name,
MEN
To the glory of Your Name,
WOMEN
To the glory of Your Name,
ALL
To the glory of Your Name.
Amen, Amen.

651 At this time of giving

(The giving song)

Words and music
Graham Kendrick

Accelerating with each verse
Dm
Gm
B♭
A7
At this time of giving, Glad - ly now we

Dm
Gm
bring Gifts of good - ness and mer - cy

B♭
A
Gm
From a heaven - ly King. Earth could not con -

Dm
A7
Dm
- tain the trea - sures Hea - ven holds for you,

Gm
Dm
B♭
A7
Per - fect joy and last - ing plea - sures, Love so strong and
1.2.3.4.
5.
Dm
Dm
true.
lai.

At this time of giving,
Gladly now we bring
Gifts of goodness and mercy
From a heavenly King.

1 Earth could not contain the treasures
Heaven holds for you,
Perfect joy and lasting pleasures,
Love so strong and true.
At this time of giving . . .

2 May His tender love surround you
At this Christmastime;
May you see His smiling face
That in the darkness shines.
At this time of giving . . .

3 But the many gifts He gives
Are all poured out from one;
Come receive the greatest gift,
The gift of God's own Son.
At this time of giving . . .

Last two choruses and verses:
Lai, lai, lai . . . *(etc.)*

652 Be still, for the presence of the Lord

Words and music
David J Evans

Unhurried
D
F♯m7
Bm
Em7
Be still, For the pres-ence of the Lord, The Ho - ly One, is
A9
A
D
F♯m7
Bm
here; Come bow be - fore Him now With
Em7
Asus
A
G
A/G
D/F♯
re - ver-ence and fear: In Him no sin is found –
G
A/G
D/F♯
G
A
We stand on ho - ly ground. Be still, For the

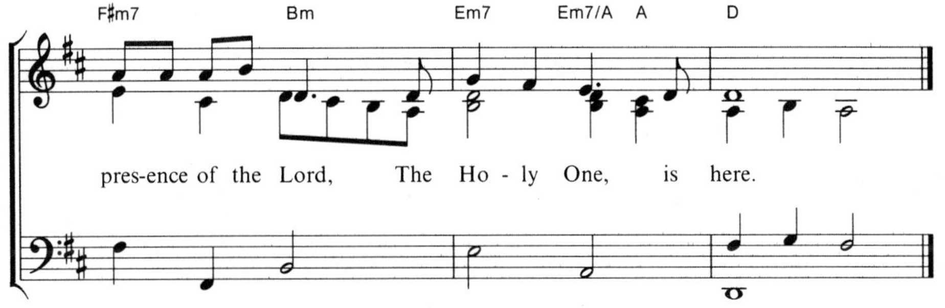
F#m7
Bm
Em7
Em7/A
A
D
pres-ence of the Lord, The Ho - ly One, is here.

1 Be still,
For the presence of the Lord,
The Holy One, is here;
Come bow before Him now
With reverence and fear:
In Him no sin is found –
We stand on holy ground.
Be still,
For the presence of the Lord,
The Holy One, is here.

2 Be still,
For the glory of the Lord
Is shining all around;
He burns with holy fire,
With splendour He is crowned:
How awesome is the sight –
Our radiant King of light!
Be still,
For the glory of the Lord
Is shining all around.

3 Be still,
For the power of the Lord
Is moving in this place:
He comes to cleanse and heal,
To minister His grace –
No work too hard for Him.
In faith receive from Him.
Be still,
For the power of the Lord
Is moving in this place.

653 Come, let us praise the Lord

66 66 44 44

Words: from Psalm 95
Timothy Dudley-Smith
Music: Chilean folk-song
adapted and arranged Michael Paget

Steadily ♩. = 54
Dm
Gm
Come, let us praise the Lord,
A7
Dm
With joy our God ac - claim,
His great-ness tell a -
Gm
A7
Dm
- broad
And bless His sav - ing Name.

If sung in harmony, the words of the bass part are the same as for the tune, but sung to the bass rhythm one syllable to each note.

Dm
C
F
Dm
Lift high your songs Be -

C
F
G
A
Dm
- fore His throne To whom a -

Gm
A7
Gm7/A A7
Dm
- lone All praise be - longs.

1 Come, let us praise the Lord,
With joy our God acclaim,
His greatness tell abroad
And bless His saving Name.
Lift high your songs
Before His throne
To whom alone
All praise belongs.

2 Our God of matchless worth,
Our King beyond compare,
The deepest bounds of earth,
The hills, are in His care.
He all decrees,
Who by His hand
Prepared the land,
And formed the seas.

3 In worship bow the knee,
Our glorious God confess;
The great Creator, He,
The Lord, our Righteousness.
He reigns unseen:
His flock He feeds
And gently leads
In pastures green.

4 Come, hear His voice today,
Receive what love imparts;
His holy will obey
And harden not your hearts.
His ways are best;
And lead at last,
All troubles past,
To perfect rest.

654 Come, let us worship

Words: from Psalm 95
Sarah Turner-Smith
Music: Paul Herrington
arranged Phil Burt

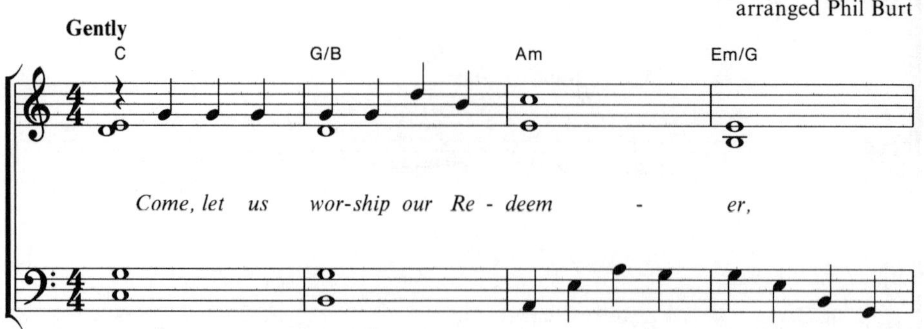
Gently
C
G/B
Am
Em/G
Come, let us wor-ship our Re - deem - er,

F
Dm
Gsus
G
C
Let us bow down be-fore His throne;
Come, let us

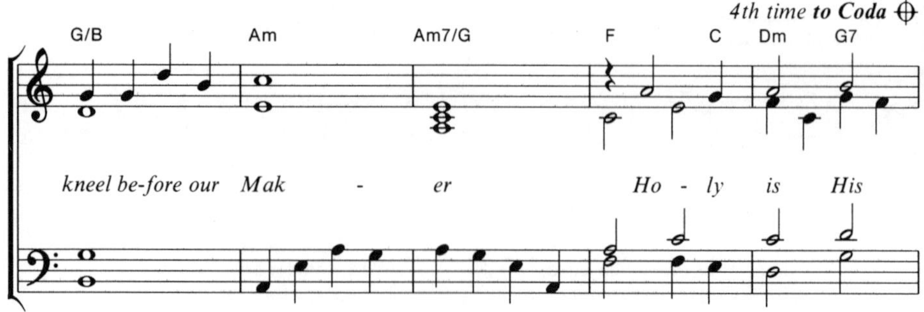
4th time to Coda
G/B
Am
Am7/G
F
C
Dm
G7
kneel be-fore our Mak - er
Ho - ly is His

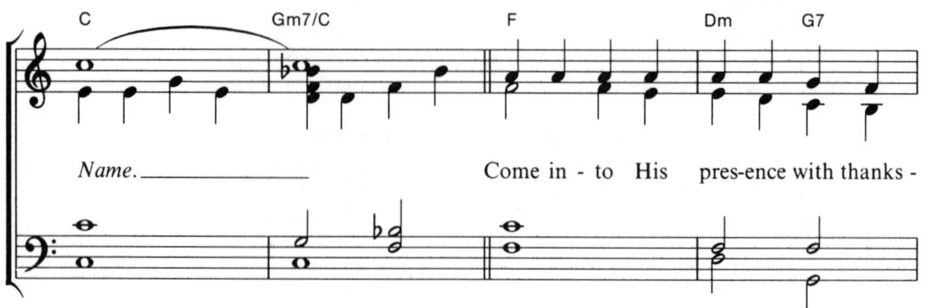
C
Gm7/C
F
Dm
G7
Name.
Come in - to His pres-ence with thanks -

Em7 Am Dm G C
-giv - ing, Make a joy - ful noise
Gm7/C F Dm7 Em7
v.2.3.
For the Lord is a great
A D Am/D F/G G7
God King a - bove all gods.
CODA
A Am/G F C/E Dm7 G7 C
Name. Ho - ly is His Name!

Come, let us worship our Redeemer,
Let us bow down before His throne;
Come, let us kneel before our Maker
Holy is His Name.

1 Come into His presence with thanksgiving,
Make a joyful noise
For the Lord is a great God
King above all gods.
Come let us worship . . .

2 We are the people of His pasture,
The sheep of His hand,
For Christ the Lord is our Shepherd,
He will lead us home.
Come let us worship . . .

3 All praises be to God the Father,
Praise to Christ His Son;
Praise be to God the Holy Spirit:
Bless the Three-in-One!
Come let us worship . . .

655 Come now with awe

Finlandia

Words: Timothy Dudley-Smith
Music: J Sibelius (1865–1957)

Capo 3(C)
E♭ (C) B♭ (G) E♭ (C) B♭7 (G7) E♭ (C) B♭7 (G7) E♭ (C) A♭ (F) B♭7 (G7) E♭ (C)
Come now with awe, earth's an-cient vi-gil keep-ing:
B♭7 (G7) E♭ (C) B♭7 (G) E♭ (C) B♭7 (G7) E♭ (C) A♭ (F) E♭ (C)
Cold un-der star-light lies the sto-ny way.
Cm (Am) E♭ (C) B♭ (G) Fm (Dm)
Down from the hill-side see the shep-herds creep-ing,
E♭/B♭ (C) A♭ (F) G (E)
Hear in our hearts the whis-pered news they say:

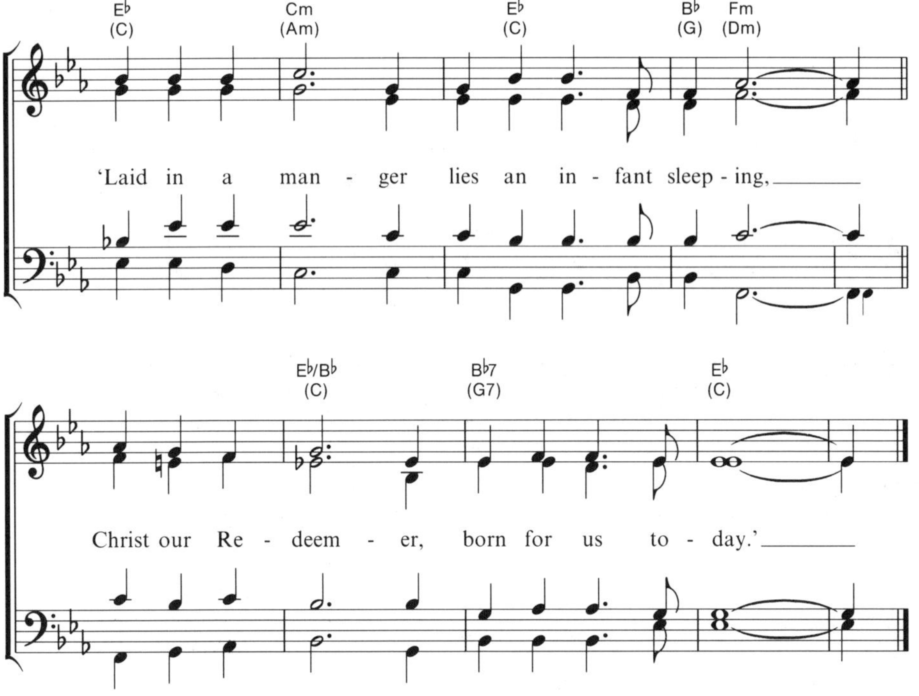
E♭
(C)
Cm
(Am)
E♭
(C)
B♭
(G)
Fm
(Dm)
'Laid in a man - ger lies an in - fant sleep - ing,
E♭/B♭
(C)
B♭7
(G7)
E♭
(C)
Christ our Re - deem - er, born for us to - day.'

1 Come now with awe, earth's ancient vigil keeping:
Cold under starlight lies the stony way.
Down from the hillside see the shepherds creeping,
Hear in our hearts the whispered news they say:
'Laid in a manger lies an infant sleeping,
Christ our Redeemer, born for us today.'

2 Come now with joy to worship and adore Him;
Hushed in the stillness, wonder and behold –
Christ in the stable where His mother bore Him,
Christ whom the prophets faithfully foretold:
High King of ages, low we kneel before Him,
Starlight for silver, lantern-light for gold.

3 Come now with faith, the age-long secret guessing,
Hearts rapt in wonder, soul and spirit stirred –
See in our likeness love beyond expressing,
All God has spoken, all the prophets heard;
Born for us sinners, bearer of all blessing,
Flesh of our flesh, behold the eternal Word!

4 Come now with love: beyond our comprehending
Love in its fullness lies in mortal span!
How should we love, whom Love is so befriending?
Love rich in mercy since our race began
Now stoops to save us, sighs and sorrows ending,
Jesus our Saviour, Son of God made man.

656 Come let us sing

Words and music
Ruth Hooke

With vigour
Bm G A Bm
WOMEN
MEN
Come let us
Come let us sing for joy to the Lord.
G A Bm
sing for joy to the Lord.
We will
G A Bm
We will
sing, we will sing, we will sing.

G
A
Bm
Fm7 Bm
sing, we will sing, we will sing.
Let us shout a - loud to the Rock
G
A
Bm
F♯m7
Bm
Let us shout a - loud to the Rock
of our sal-va - tion.
G
A
G
A
of our sal-va - tion.
We will shout! We will shout! We will

Bm
G
A
Bm
We will shout! We will shout! We will shout!
For the
shout!
For the
f
A
Bm
A
Lord is the_ great God,_ the great King a - bove all 3
Lord is the_ great God,_ the great King a - bove all 3
3
Gmaj7
F♯m7
Bm
F♯m7
gods.
Splen-dour and
gods.
Splen-dour and maj-es-ty,
8va

Bm
F♯m7
maj-es-ty,
Are be - fore
Are be - fore
Him,
G
A
Him.
Strength
and
Strength
and
glo
-
ry,
8va bassa
Bm
A
Bm
glo - ry, Are in His
sanc
-
tua
-
ry.
Are in His
sanc
-
tua
-
ry.

657 Child in the manger

Words: after M MacDonald (1789–1872)
L Macbean (1853–1931)
Music: Gaelic melody
arranged Phil Burt

Gently
D Bm G A E A Bm
Child in the man - ger, in - fant of Ma - ry, Out - cast and

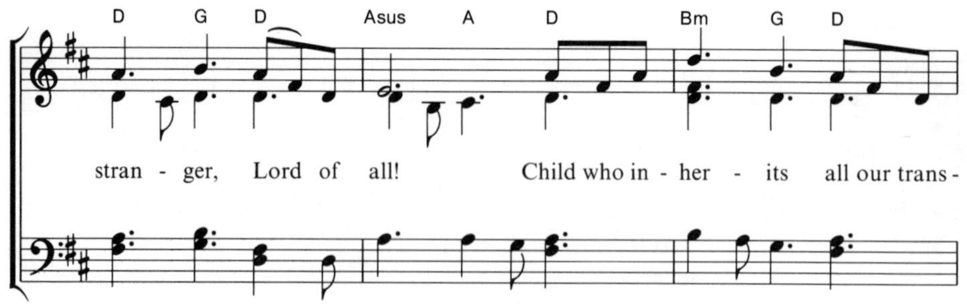
D G D Asus A D Bm G D
stran - ger, Lord of all! Child who in - her - its all our trans -

Bm G D F♯m Bm G A7 D
- gres - sions, All our de - mer - its on Him fall.

1 Child in the manger, infant of Mary,
Outcast and stranger, Lord of all!
Child who inherits all our transgressions,
All our demerits on Him fall.

2 Once the most holy child of salvation
Gentle and lowly lived below:
Now as our glorious mighty Redeemer,
See Him victorious over each foe.

3 Prophets foretold Him, infant of wonder;
Angels behold Him on His throne:
Worthy our Saviour of all their praises;
Happy for ever are His own.

658 Darkness like a shroud

Arise, Shine

Words and music
Graham Kendrick

Subdued, becoming bright
Capo 4(C)
C♯m (Am) B/C♯ (G/A) C♯m (Am) A (F) B (G) E (C)
1 Dark - ness like a shroud Co - vers the earth,
2 Child - ren of the light, Be clean and pure;
3 Here a - mong us now, Christ the Light
4 Like a ci - ty bright, So let us blaze;
C♯m (Am) B/C♯ (G/A) C♯m (Am) A (F) B (G) G♯sus (Esus) G♯ (E)
E - vil like a cloud Co - vers the peo-ple; But the
Rise, you sleep - ers, Christ will shine on you: Take the
Kin - dles bright-er flames In our tremb-ling hearts: Liv-ing
Lights in ev - ery street Turn - ing night to day: And the
E (C) F♯m7 (Dm7) B (G) E (C) F♯m7 (Dm7)
Lord will rise up - on you, And His glo - ry will ap -
Spi - rit's flash - ing two-edged sword And with faith de - clare God's
Word, our lamp, come guide our feet As we walk as one in
dark - ness shall not ov - er - come, Till the full - ness of Christ's
B (G) E (C) C♯m7 (Am7) F♯m (Dm)
- pear on you, Na - tions will come to your
migh - ty word; Stand up, and in His strength be
light and peace, Jus - tice and truth shine like the
king - dom comes, Dawn - ing to God's e - ter - nal

Bsus (Gsus) B (G) F♯m/B (Dm/G) B (G) E (C) G♯m (Em) C♯m (Am) G♯m (Em) C♯m (Am)
light.
strong!
sun.
day.
A - rise, shine, your light has come, The
A (F) F♯m (Dm) A/B (F/G) E (C) G♯m (Em)
glo - ry of the Lord has risen on you; a - rise, shine, your
A (F) G♯m (Em) Amaj7 (Fmaj7) A♯dim (F♯dim) E/B (C/G) G♯m (Em)
light has come – Je - sus the light of the
1.2.3.
4.
A (F) A/B (F/G) E (C) G♯7 (E7) A (F) A♯dim (F♯dim) E/B (C/G) G♯m (Em)
world has come. world, Je-sus the light of the
A (F) A♯dim (F♯dim) E/B (C/G) G♯m (Em) A (F) A/B (F/G) E (C)
world, Je-sus the light of the world has come.

659 Emmanuel, Emmanuel

Words and music
Bob McGee

With warmth
C F G7 C
Em-man - u - el, Em-man - u - el,
A7 Dm Dm7 G7 C
His name is called Em-man - u - el
F G7 Em
God with us, Re-vealed in us
A7 Dm Dm7 G7 C
His name is called Em-man - u - el.

Emmanuel, Emmanuel,
His name is called Emmanuel –
God with us,
Revealed in us –
His name is called Emmanuel.

660 Faithful vigil ended

Faithful Vigil

Words: from Luke 2
Timothy Dudley-Smith
Music: David Wilson

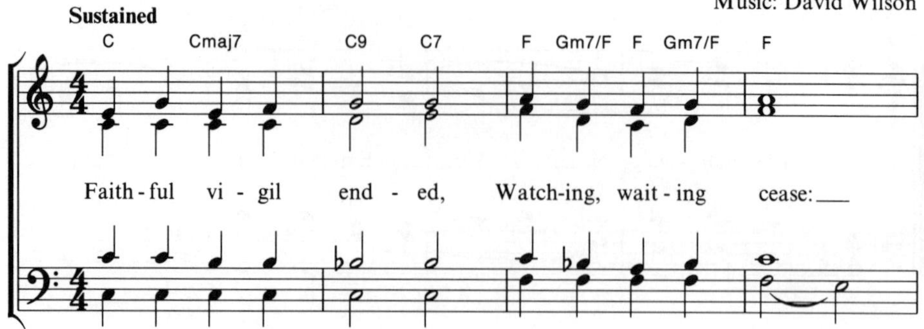

Sustained
C Cmaj7 C9 C7 F Gm7/F F Gm7/F F
Faith - ful vi - gil end - ed, Watch-ing, wait - ing cease:

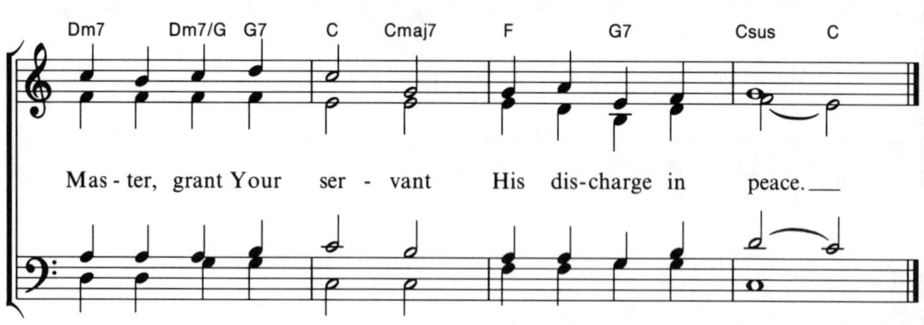

Dm7 Dm7/G G7 C Cmaj7 F G7 Csus C
Mas - ter, grant Your ser - vant His dis-charge in peace.

1 Faithful vigil ended,
Watching, waiting cease:
Master, grant Your servant
His discharge in peace.

2 All the Spirit promised,
All the Father willed,
Now these eyes behold it
Perfectly fulfilled.

3 This Your great deliverance
Sets Your people free;
Christ their light uplifted
All the nations see.

4 Christ, Your people's glory!
Watching, doubting cease:
Grant to us Your servants
Our discharge in peace.

661 Father in heaven how we love You

Words and music
Bob Fitts

Majestically
C
Cmaj7
Dm
G7
Fa-ther in hea-ven, how we love You,
We lift Your Name in all the
C
Fmaj/G
C
Cmaj7
Dm
earth.
May Your king-dom be es-tab-lished in our prais-es
As Your
Dm/G
G7
C
G7
C
Cmaj7
peo-ple dec-lare Your migh-ty works.
Bless-èd be the Lord God Al-
Dm
G7
C
G7
-migh-ty,
Who was and is and is to come,
Bless-èd be the
C
Cmaj7
Dm7
G7
C
Lord God Al-migh-ty,
Who reigns for ev-er-more.

662 Father in heaven

We will crown Him

Words and music
Dave Bilbrough

Rhythmic
Capo 3(Am)
Cm (Am)
G (E)
Ab (F)
Eb (C)
Bb (G)
1 Fa-ther in___ hea - ven, Our voi-ces we raise: Re-ceive our de - vo-tion, Re-ceive now our praise As we sing of the glo - ry Of all that You've done – The great-est love-sto - ry That's ev - er been sung.
2 Fa-ther in___ hea - ven, Our lives are Your own; We've been caught by a vi-sion Of Je - sus a - lone – Who_ came as a ser - vant To free us from sin: Fa-ther in_ hea-ven, Our wor-ship we bring.
(3) sing_ Al - le - lu - ia, We will sing to the King, To our migh-ty De - li-verer Our al-le - lu - ias will ring. Yes, our praise is re - sound-ing To the Lamb on the throne: He a - lone_ is ex-al - ted Through the love He has shown.

Cm
(Am)
B♭
(G)
Cm
(Am)
B♭
(G)
And we will crown You Lord of all, Yes, we will crown You Lord of
Cm
(Am)
A♭
(F)
B♭
(G)
G
(E)
Cm
(Am)
B♭
(G)
all, For You have won the vic-to-ry: Yes, we will crown You Lord of
1.
Cm
(Am)
all.
2.
Cm
(Am)
all.
3 We will
3.
Cm
(Am)
all.

1 Father in heaven,
Our voices we raise:
Receive our devotion,
Receive now our praise
As we sing of the glory
Of all that You've done –
The greatest love-story
That's ever been sung.
And we will crown You Lord of all,
Yes, we will crown You Lord of all,
For You have won the victory:
Yes, we will crown You Lord of all.

2 Father in heaven,
Our lives are Your own;
We've been caught by a vision
Of Jesus alone –
Who came as a servant
To free us from sin:
Father in heaven,
Our worship we bring.
And we will crown . . .

3 We will sing Alleluia,
We will sing to the King,
To our mighty Deliverer
Our alleluias will ring.
Yes, our praise is resounding
To the Lamb on the throne:
He alone is exalted
Through the love He has shown.
And we will crown . . .

663 Father, never was love so near

(Thanks be to God)

Words and music
Graham Kendrick

Smoothly, not too slow
B/A A B/A A D/A B Esus/B

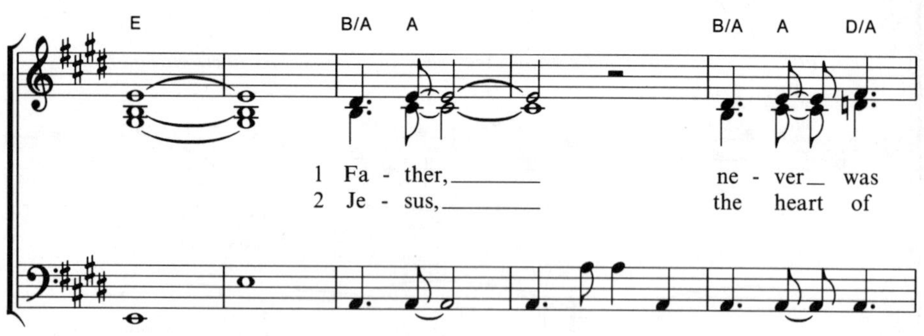
E B/A A B/A A D/A
1 Fa - ther, ne - ver was
2 Je - sus, the heart of

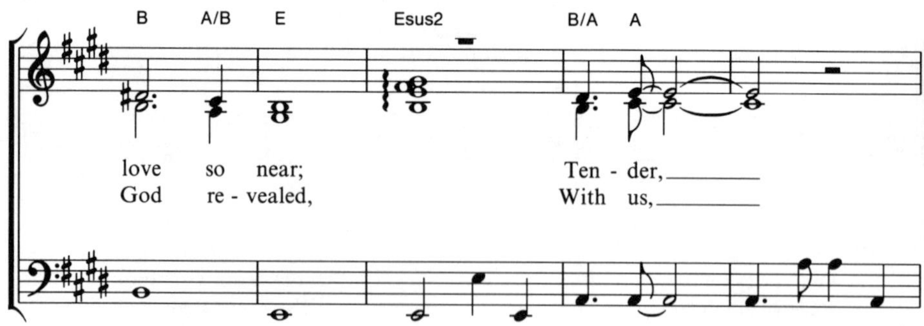
B A/B E Esus2 B/A A
love so near; Ten - der,
God re - vealed, With us,

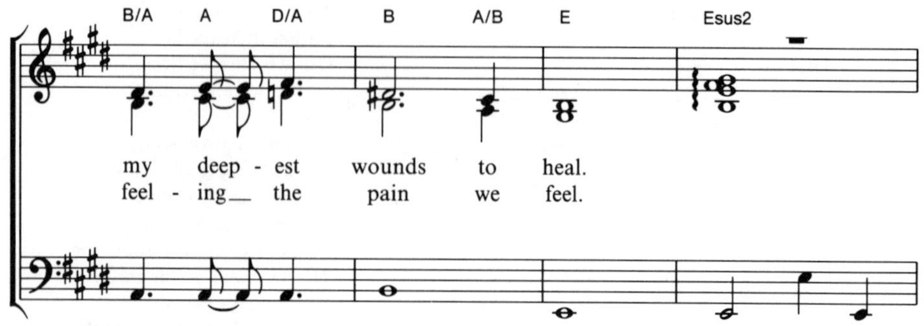
B/A A D/A B A/B E Esus2
my deep - est wounds to heal.
feel - ing the pain we feel.

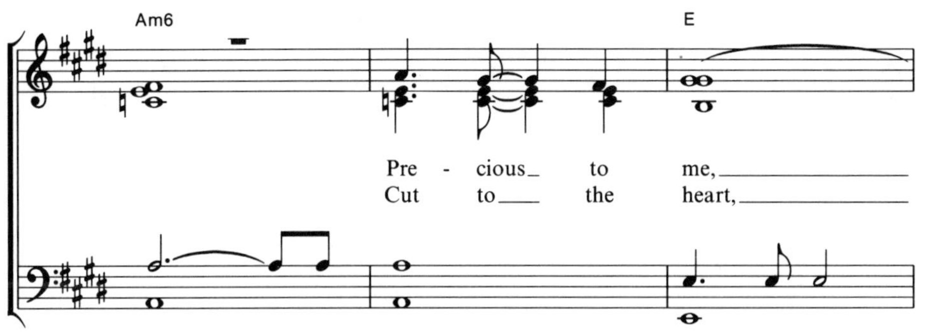
Am6
E
Pre - cious to me,
Cut to the heart,

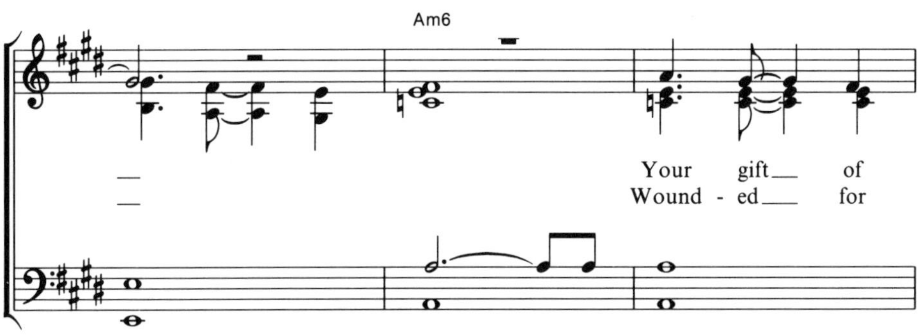
Am6
Your gift of
Wound - ed for

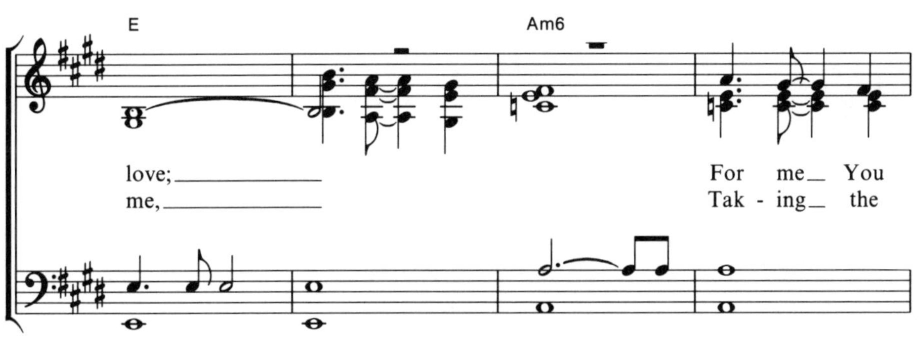
E
Am6
love;
me,
For me You
Tak - ing the

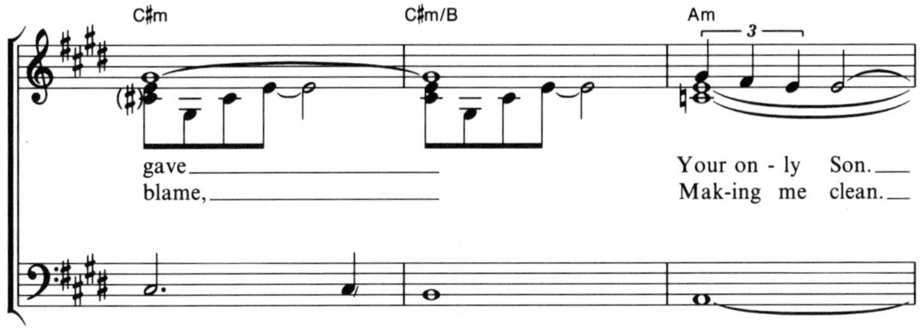
C♯m
C♯m/B
Am
3
gave
blame,
Your on - ly Son.
Mak-ing me clean.

B
E
Emaj7
Bm7
And now
C♯7
F♯m
F♯m(maj7)
F♯m7
thanks be to God
For His
Am
E
Emaj7
Bm7
gift be - yond words,
The
C♯7
F♯m
F♯m(maj7)
F♯m7
Son whom He loved,
No, He
Am
E
C♯m
F♯m
did not with - hold
Him,
But

Am6
G♯m7
C♯m
Am6
with Him_ gave ev - ery - thing. Now He's ev - ery -
B6
1.
E
D.C. to next verse
2.
E
- thing to me. me.
D.𝄋
3.
C♯m
C♯m/B
And me, now
rall.
Am6
B6
a tempo
E
Esus
rit.
E
He's ev - ery - thing to me.

1 Father, never was love so near;
Tender, my deepest wounds to heal.
Precious to me,
Your gift of love;
For me You gave
Your only Son.
And now thanks be to God
For His gift beyond words,
The Son whom He loved,
No, He did not withhold Him,
But with Him gave everything.
Now He's everything to me.

2 Jesus, the heart of God revealed,
With us, feeling the pain we feel.
Cut to the heart,
Wounded for me,
Taking the blame,
Making me clean.
And now thanks be to God . . .

664 For God so loved the world

Words and music
Graham Kendrick

Smoothly
Capo 2(D)
E (D)
Emaj7 (Dmaj7)
F♯m7 (Em7)
A/B (G)
B (A)
WOMEN 1 For
E (D)
Emaj7 (Dmaj7)
F♯m (Em)
F♯m7 (Em7)
God so loved the world That He
B7 (A)
Cdim (A♯dim)
E (D)
F♯m (Em)
A/B (G)
gave His on - ly Son; And
E (D)
Emaj7 (Dmaj7)
F♯m (Em)
F♯m7 (Em7)
all who be-lieve in Him Shall not

Am (Gm)
F♯m7/B (Em7)
G♯m7 (F♯m7)
C♯m (Bm)
die, But have e - ter - nal life; No, they shall not
2nd time to Coda
F♯m7 (Em)
A/B (G)
B (A)
E (D)
A/E (G)
E (D)
die, But have e - ter - nal life.
ALL 2 And
CODA
E (D)
G♯m7 (F♯m7)
C♯m7 (Bm7)
life.
1.2.
3.
F♯m7 (Em7)
A/B (G)
B (A)
A/B (G)
B (A)
E (D)

WOMEN

1 For God so loved the world
That He gave His only Son;
And all who believe in Him
Shall not die,
But have eternal life;
No, they shall not die,
But have eternal life.

ALL

2 And God showed His love for you,
When He gave His only Son;
And you, if you trust in Him,
Shall not die,
But have eternal life;
No you shall not die,
But have eternal life.

665 For unto us a child is born

Words and music
David J Hadden

Flowing and expressive
C
Cmaj7
1 For un - to us a child is born, Un - to
(2) there shall be no end To the
(3) is the Migh - ty God, He
F9
Gsus
us a son is given, And the gov - ern - ment shall
in - crease of His rule, To the in - crease of His
is the Prince of peace, The King of kings and
G7
C
G7
be up - on His shoul - der; For un - to
gov - ern - ment and peace; For He shall
Lord of lords: All
C
Cmaj7
F9
us a child is born, Un - to us a son is given,
sit on Da - vid's throne Up - hold - ing right - eous-ness,
hon - our to the King, All glo - ry to His name,

Gsus G7 C
And the gov-ern-ment shall be up-on His shoul - der.
Our God shall ac - comp-lish this.
For now and for ev - er-more!
G7 C F
And He will be called Won-der-ful, Won-der-ful Coun-sel-lor,
Dm G C
Migh - - - ty God,
Gsus G C F Dm
The Ev-er-last - ing Fa-ther, Prince of peace,
C/G G7 1.2. C Gsus G 3. C
Migh - - - ty God.
2 And
3 For He

666 From the sun's rising

Words and music
Graham Kendrick
Steadily
Capo 2(C)
D (C) G (F) D (C) A (G) D (C) G (F)
1 From the sun's ris - ing Un - to the sun's set-ting Je - sus our Lord Shall be
2 To ev - ery tongue, tribe And na - tion He sends us, To make di - sci - ples, To
3 Come let us join with The church from all nations, Cross ev - ery bor - der, Throw
D (C) Asus (Gsus) A (G) D (C) G (F) D (C) A (G)
great in the earth; And all earth's kingdoms Shall be His do - mi - nion –
teach and bap - tize; For all au - tho - ri - ty To Him is gi - ven
wide ev - ery door; Workers with Him As He ga - thers His har-vest,
D (C) G (F) Bm (Am) G/A (F) A7 (G7) D (C) Dsus (Csus) D (C)
All of cre - a - tion Shall sing of His worth.
Now as His wit - nes - ses We shall a - rise.
Till earth's far cor-ners Our Sav - iour a - dore.
Bm (Am) F♯m (Em) G (F) D (C) Em (Dm)
Let ev - ery heart, ev - ery voice, Ev - ery tongue join with spi - rits a -

Asus
(Gsus)
A
(G)
Bm
(Am)
F♯m
(Em)
G
(F)
D
(C)
-blaze; One in His love, We will cir - cle the world With the
Em
(Dm)
F♯sus
(Esus)
F♯
(E)
Em7
(Dm7)
A
(G)
song of His praise. O let all His peo - ple re -
last time to Coda
Bm
(Am)
G
(F)
A
(G)
D
(C)
Dsus
(Csus)
D
(C)
Asus
(Gsus)
A
(G)
-joice, And let all the earth hear His voice!
CODA
Bm
(Am)
Em
(Dm)
A
(G)
Bm
(Am)
voice! Let all His peo - ple re - joice,
G
(F)
A
(G)
D
(C)
Dsus
(Csus)
D
(C)
And let all the earth hear His voice!

667 Give thanks to the Lord

(His love endures forever)

Words and music
Mark Hayes

Capo 3(D)
F
(D)
1 Give thanks to the Lord for He is good,
(2) un - der - stand - ing made the heavens,
(3) child - ren through the wil - der - ness.
(4) - mem-bered us in our low es - tate
His

B♭
(G)
F/C
(D/A)
C
(A)
F
(D)
love en - dures for ev - er.
Give thanks to the God
Who made the great and shin -
And struck down ma - ny migh -
And freed us from our en -

B♭
(G)
F/C
(D/A)
C
(A)
of gods.
- ing lights,
- ty kings,
- e - mies.
His love en - dures for ev - er.
The
And
To

B♭ (G)
F/A (D/F♯)
Gm (Em) F/A (D/F♯) Gm/B♭ (Em/G) G7/B (E7/G♯)
O give thanks to the Lord of lords.
migh - ty sun to rule the day,
gave to them an in - he - ri - tance,
ev - ery crea - ture He gives food.
His love en - dures for

F/C (D/A)
C (A)
F (D)
F/E♭ (D/C)
C/D (A/B)
ev - er.
To Him a - lone who does great works.
And the moon and the stars to rule at night.
A pro-mised land for Is - ra - el.
Give thanks to the God of heaven.
His

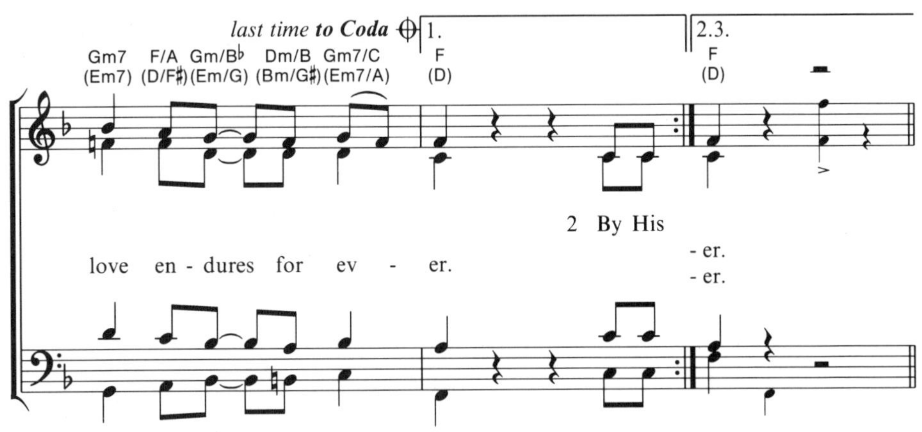
last time to Coda
1.
2.3.
Gm7 (Em7) F/A (D/F♯) Gm/B♭ (Em/G) Dm/B (Bm/G♯) Gm7/C (Em7/A)
F (D)
F (D)
2 By His
love en - dures for ev - er.
- er.
- er.

Dm
(Bm)
C
(A)
F
(D)
E♭
(C)
E♭/D♭
(C/B♭)
Hal - le - lu - jah, Hal - le - lu, The Lord Je - ho - vah
Csus
(Asus)
C
(A)
B♭
(G)
C/B♭
(A/G)
F/A
(D/F♯)
Dm7
(Bm7)
reigns. He is the same_ from age to___ age; His
Gm7
(Em7)
F/A
(D/F♯)
Gm/B♭
(Em/G)
Gm7/C
(Em7/A)
F
(D)
love will ne - ver change. 3 God_ led His
4 He re -
CODA
F
(D)
Gm7
(Em7)
F/A
(D/F♯)
Gm/B♭
(Em/G)
Dm/B
(Bm/G♯)
Gm7/C
(Em7/A)
F
(D)
- er. His love en - dures for ev - er. His

Gm7
(Em7)
F/A
(D/F♯)
Gm/B♭
(Em/G)
Gm7
(Em7)
Gm/C
(Em/A)
love en - dures for ev - -
F
(D)
B♭
(G)
F/A
(D/F♯)
B♭
(G)
C
(A)
B♭/C
(G/A)
- er.
rall.

1 Give thanks to the Lord for He is good,
His love endures for ever.
Give thanks to the God of gods.
His love endures for ever.
O give thanks to the Lord of lords.
His love endures for ever.
To Him alone who does great works.
His love endures for ever.

2 By His understanding made the heavens,
His love endures for ever.
Who made the great and shining lights,
His love endures for ever.
The mighty sun to rule the day,
His love endures for ever.
And the moon and the stars to rule at night.
His love endures for ever.
Hallelujah, Hallelu,
The Lord Jehovah reigns.
He is the same from age to age;
His love will never change.

3 God led His children through the wilderness.
His love endures for ever.
And struck down many mighty kings,
His love endures for ever.
And gave to them an inheritance,
His love endures for ever.
A promised land for Israel.
His love endures for ever.
Hallelujah . . .

4 He remembered us in our low estate
His love endures for ever.
And freed us from our enemies.
His love endures for ever.
To every creature He gives food.
His love endures for ever.
Give thanks to the God of heaven.
His love endures for ever.
His love endures for ever.
His love endures for ever.

668 Glory

Words and music
Danny Daniels

Bright, joyful
G C G
Glo - ry, glo - ry in the high - est, Glo - ry,
C G D C
to the Al - migh - ty; Glo-ry to the Lamb of God,___ And
G D C G D
glo - ry to the liv - ing Word;___ Glo - ry___
C D G 1. 2.3. G
to the Lamb! MEN: I give

C
G
glo - ry ___ WOMEN: Glo - ry ___
MEN: Glo - ry ___ WOMEN: Glo - ry ___
A
D
1.3.
MEN: Glo - ry ___
ALL: Glo-ry to the ___ Lamb! ___
MEN: I give
2nd time to Coda
D.𝄋 al Coda
2.4.
G D C D G
ALL: I give glo - ry to ___ the Lamb!
CODA
D G D C D G
I give glo - ry to ___ the Lamb!

669 God of all ages

Words: Philip Coutts
Music: Peter Graham

Capo 5(C)
F (C) C (G) F (C) Dm (Am) Gm (Dm) Asus (Esus) A7 (E7)
God of all a - ges and Lord for all time, Cre -
Dm (Am) Dm7/C (Am7/G) G/B (D/F♯) E7 (B7) Am (Em)
-a - tor of all things in per - fect de - sign: For
Cm (Gm) Gm (Dm) B♭m (Fm) B♭m9/G (Fm9/C) B♭m (Fm)
fields ripe for har - vest, for rich gold - en grain, For
F/C (C/G) Fmaj7/C (Cmaj7/G) G7/C (D7/G) B♭/C (F/G) C7 (G7) F (C)
beau - ty in na - ture, we thank You a - gain.

The guitar chords are not compatible with the piano accompaniment

1 God of all ages and Lord for all time,
Creator of all things in perfect design:
For fields ripe for harvest, for rich golden grain,
For beauty in nature, we thank You again.

2 God of all nations and Lord of all lands,
Who placed the world's wealth in the palm of our hands,
We pray for Your guidance to guard against greed.
Though great the resources, still great is the need.

3 God of compassion and Lord of all life,
We pray for Your people in conflict and strife.
The earth You created a vast treasure store,
Yet hunger still thrives while men fight to gain more.

4 God of all wisdom, take us by the hand
And insight bestow when we ruin Your land.
For rivers polluted, for forests laid bare,
We pray Your forgiveness for failing to care.

5 God of all greatness and giver of light,
With each sunlit morning we worship Your might,
Our half-hearted service Your only reward:
For love beyond measure, we thank You O Lord.

670 Glorious Father

Words and music
Danny Reed

C F/C C F C
Glo - ri - ous Fa-ther we ex - alt__ You. We wor - ship, hon-our and a -
G7 Am Am/G♯ Am/G D9
- dore_ You. We de - light to be_ in Your pres - ence O Lord. We
G9 G7 C G C G/B
mag - ni - fy__ Your Ho - ly Name, And we sing come Lord
Am Gm7 C9 F G7 C G
Je - sus, Glo - ri - fy Your Name, And we sing
C G/B Am Gm7 C9 F G7 C
come Lord Je - sus, Glo - ri - fy Your Name.

671 Great is the Lord

Words and music
Steve McEwan

Worshipfully
Capo 2(G)
A
(G)
D/A
(C/G)
Great is the Lord and most wor-thy of
A
(G)
D/A
(C/G)
F♯m
(Em)
praise, The ci-ty of our God, the ho-ly place, The
A/E
(G/D)
Bm7
(Am7)
Bm7 C♯m7 Dmaj7 D/E
(Am7) (Bm7) (Cmaj7) (C/D)
joy of the whole earth.
A
(G)
D/A
(C/G)
Great is the Lord in whom we have the vic - to-ry,

A
(G)
D/A
(C/G)
F♯m
(Em)
— He aids us a-gainst the e - ne - my, We
A/E
(G/D)
Bm7
(Am7)
D/E
(C/D)
E
(D)
D/F♯
(C/E)
E/G♯
(D/F♯)
bow down on — our knees. — And
A
(G)
C♯m7
(Bm7)
Lord, we want to lift — Your name on high, And
D
(C)
A/C♯
(G/B)
Bm7
(Am7)
D/E
(C/D)
Lord, we want to thank You, For the works You've done in our lives; And

A
(G)
C♯m7
(Bm7)
Lord, we trust in Your un - fail - ing love, For
D
(C)
A/C♯
(G/B)
Bm7
(Am7)
D/E
(C/D)
You a - lone are God e - ter - nal, Through-out earth and hea-ven a -
last time only
A
(G)
D/A
(C/G)
A
(G)
- bove.

Great is the Lord and most worthy of praise,
The city of our God, the holy place,
The joy of the whole earth.
Great is the Lord in whom we have the victory,
He aids us against the enemy,
We bow down on our knees.

And Lord, we want to lift Your name on high,
And Lord, we want to thank You,
For the works You've done in our lives;
And Lord, we trust in Your unfailing love,
For You alone are God eternal,
Throughout earth and heaven above.

672 Go, tell it on the mountain

Words and music
Geoffrey Marshall-Taylor
Music arranged Douglas Coombes

Brightly
G C G C G D7
Go, tell it on the moun - tain, O-ver the hills and ev-ery-where;
G C G C D7 G
Fine
Go, tell it on the moun - tain That Je-sus is His Name.
G Em C G
He pos-sessed no rich-es, no home to lay His head; He
G Em C D
D.C. al Fine
saw the needs of oth-ers and cared for them in - stead.

Go, tell it on the mountain,
Over the hills and everywhere;
Go, tell it on the mountain
That Jesus is His Name.

1 He possessed no riches, no home to lay His head;
He saw the needs of others and cared for them instead.
Go tell it on the mountain . . .

2 He reached out and touched them, the blind, the deaf, the lame;
He spoke and listened gladly to anyone who came.
Go tell it on the mountain . . .

3 Some turned away in anger, with hatred in the eye;
They tried Him and condemned Him, then led Him out to die.
Go tell it on the mountain . . .

4 'Father, now forgive them' – those were the words He said;
In three more days He was alive and risen from the dead.
Go tell it on the mountain . . .

5 He still comes to people, His life moves through the lands;
He uses us for speaking, He touches with our hands.
Go tell it on the mountain . . .

673 God came among us

Words and music
Marilyn Baker
Music arranged Phil Burt

C
G
God came a - mong us, He be - came a man,
Dm
A7
Dm
G
Be-came a ba - by, though through Him the world be - gan.
Am
D
G
C/E
He came to earth to bring us peace, But
F
Dm
G
G7
where is that peace to - day?
It can be found

C
Am
Dm
F/G
G
1.2.
C
G/B
— By— those who will let Him dir-ect their— way.
Am
D/F♯
G7/F
C/E
Dm
G
3.
C
- lieve.

1 God came among us, He became a man,
Became a baby, though through Him the world began.
He came to earth to bring us peace,
But where is that peace today?
It can be found
By those who will let Him direct their way.

2 He came to serve, to show us how much He cared;
Our joys and sorrows He so willingly shared.
He came to earth to bring us joy,
But where is that joy today?
It can be found
By those who let Him wash their guilt away.

3 Death tried to hold Him, but it could not succeed;
He rose again, and now we can be freed.
He longs to give eternal life
To all who will simply receive,
Yes to all who
Will open their hearts and just believe.

674 'Hallelujah', sing to the Lord

(Ancient of days)

Words and music
Steve and Gina Southworth

With a swing
G D/G C/G D/G G D
'Hal - le - lu - jah' sing to the Lord
stretch out our hands, we stretch out our hands un -
G D G D C D
songs of praise; We bless You, Lord, We
- to You, Lord; We lift up our voice, We
G D G D 1. G
give to You glo - ry due Your ho - ly Name.
lift up our voice in - vit - ing You in - to this
C D G 2. G C D G
We place.

G
C
G
C
G
Hear us, O God; As one, we bring our
D
G
C
G
C
G
praise. A pleas - ing sac - ri - fice to You, O An-cient of
D
Dsus
D
G
C
D
G
Days; An-cient of Days.

'Hallelujah' sing to the Lord songs of praise;
We bless You, Lord,
We give to You glory due Your holy Name.
We stretch out our hands, we stretch out our hands unto You, Lord;
We lift up our voice,
We lift up our voice inviting You into this place.
Hear us, O God;
As one, we bring our praise.
A pleasing sacrifice to You,
O Ancient of Days;
Ancient of Days.

675 He has shown you

Words and music
Graham Kendrick

Steadily
Em7
Asus
A
He has shown you, O man, what is good — And

Em7
Asus
A
Em7
what does the Lord re-quire of you? He has shown you, O man, what is

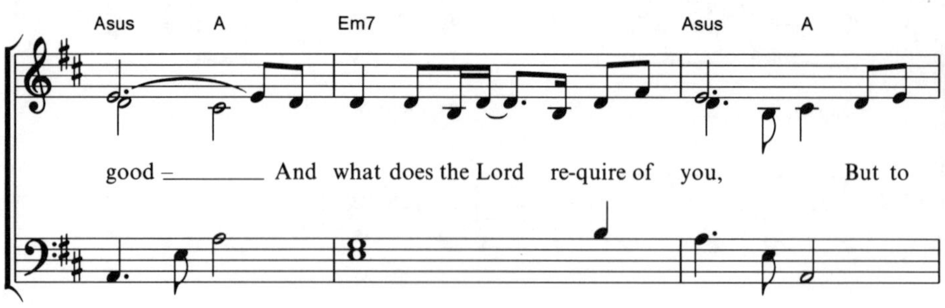
Asus
A
Em7
Asus
A
good — And what does the Lord re-quire of you, But to

D
G/D
D
G
D
Bm
act just-ly, and to love mer-cy, And to walk hum-bly with your

Em7
A
D
G/D
D
G
God; But to act just-ly, and to love mer-cy, And to

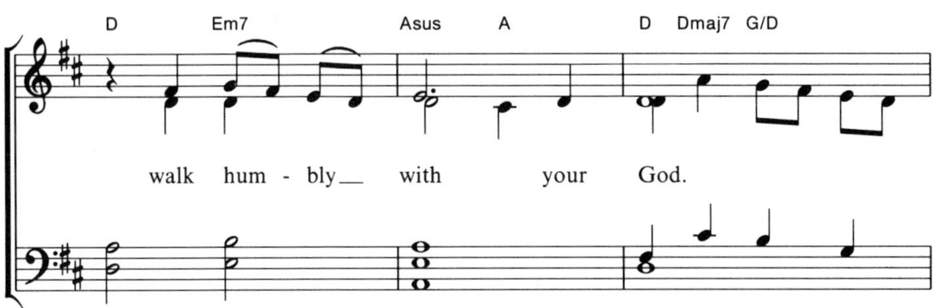
D
Em7
Asus
A
D
Dmaj7
G/D
walk hum - bly__ with your God.

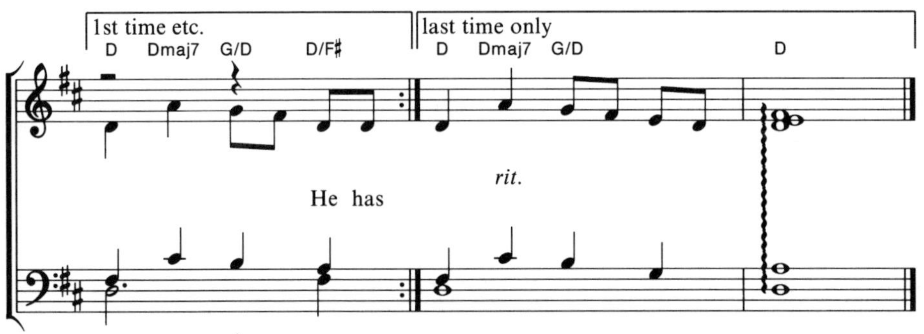
1st time etc.
D
Dmaj7
G/D
D/F♯
last time only
D
Dmaj7
G/D
D
He has
rit.

He has shown you, O man, what is good –
And what does the Lord require of you?
He has shown you, O man, what is good –
And what does the Lord require of you,
But to act justly, and to love mercy,
And to walk humbly with your God;
But to act justly, and to love mercy,
And to walk humbly with your God.
He has shown . . .

676 He is born, our Lord and Saviour

Words and music
Jimmy Owens

Joyfully
Capo 2(D)
E (D) C♯m (Bm) F♯m (Em) B7 (A7) E (D)
He is born, our Lord___ and Sav - iour:
B7/D♯ (A7/C♯) E (D) B7/F♯ (A7/E) E (D) F♯m (Em) F♯7 (E7) B (A) E (D) C♯m (Bm)
He is born, our heaven - ly King: Give Him hon - our,
F♯m (Em) B7 (A7) E (D) B7/D♯ (A7/C♯) E (D) B7/F♯ (A7/E) E (D) F♯m (Em) B7 (A7) E (D)
give__ Him glo - ry, Earth re - joice and hea - ven sing!
E7 (D7) C♯ (B) F♯m (Em) B (A)
Born to be our sanc - tu - ar - y,___

E
(D)
A
(G)
F♯/A♯
(E/G♯)
F♯7
(E7)
B7
(A7)
Born to bring_ us_ light_ and peace;
E/G♯
(D/F♯)
C♯m
(Bm)
F♯m
(Em)
B7
(A7)
E
(D)
E/G♯
(D/F♯)
For our sins to bring_ for - give - ness,
A
(G)
B7/F♯
(A7/E)
E/G♯
(D/F♯)
C♯m
(Bm)
F♯m
(Em)
B7
(A7)
E
(D)
From our_ guilt_ to bring_ re - lease.

1 He is born, our Lord and Saviour:
He is born, our heavenly King:
Give Him honour, give Him glory,
Earth rejoice and heaven sing!
Born to be our sanctuary,
Born to bring us light and peace;
For our sins to bring forgiveness,
From our guilt to bring release.

2 He who is from everlasting
Now becomes the incarnate Word;
He whose name endures for ever
Now is born the Son of God:
Born to bear our griefs and sorrows,
Born to banish hate and strife;
Born to bear the sin of many,
Born to give eternal life!

3 Hail, the holy One of Israel,
Chosen heir to David's throne;
Hail the brightness of His rising –
To His light the gentiles come:
Plunderer of Satan's kingdom,
Downfall of his evil power;
Rescuer of all His people,
Conqueror in death's dark hour!

4 He shall rule with righteous judgement,
And His godly rule extend;
Governor among the nations,
His great kingdom has no end:
He shall reign, the King of glory,
Higher than the kings of earth –
Alleluia, alleluia!
Praise we now His holy birth!

677 He is exalted

Words and music
Twila Paris
Capo 3(D) F (D)
F/A (D/F♯)
B♭ (G)
He is ex - alt - ed, The King is ex - alt - ed on high. I will
B♭/D (G/B)
C/E (A/C♯)
F (D)
F/A (D/F♯)
praise Him. He is ex - alt - ed, For ev - er ex - alt - ed And
B♭ (G)
C/B♭ (A/G)
B♭/C (G/A)
Dsus (Bsus)
D/C (B/A)
I will praise His Name!
Gm (Em)
Dm/F (Bm/D)
C/E (A/C♯)
C (A)
F (D)
Am7 (F♯m7)
He is the Lord. For ev - er His truth shall

B♭ (G) F/A (D/F♯) Gm (Em) Dm/F (Bm/D) C/E (A/C♯) Gm/D (Em/B) C (A)
reign. Hea - ven and earth Re -
F (D) Am7 (F♯m7) B♭ (G) F/A (D/F♯) Gm (Em) Gm/F (Em/D)
-joice in His ho - ly Name. He is ex - alt - ed, The
E♭maj9 (Cmaj9) Gm7/C (Em7/A) F (D)
King is ex - alt - ed on high.

He is exalted,
The King is exalted on high.
I will praise Him.
He is exalted,
For ever exalted
And I will praise His Name!

He is the Lord.
For ever His truth shall reign.
Heaven and earth
Rejoice in His holy Name.
He is exalted,
The King is exalted on high.

678 He walked where I walk

(God with us)

Words and music
Graham Kendrick

Quite quick, with a steady rhythm
Csus
C
Csus2
C
Repeat 3 times
G
Am
F/C
LEADER
ALL
1 He walked where I____ walk,
2 One of a ha - ted race,
He walked where I____ walk,
One of a ha - ted race,
He stood where I____ stand,
Stung by the pre - ju - dice,
He stood where I____ stand,
Stung by the pre - ju - dice,

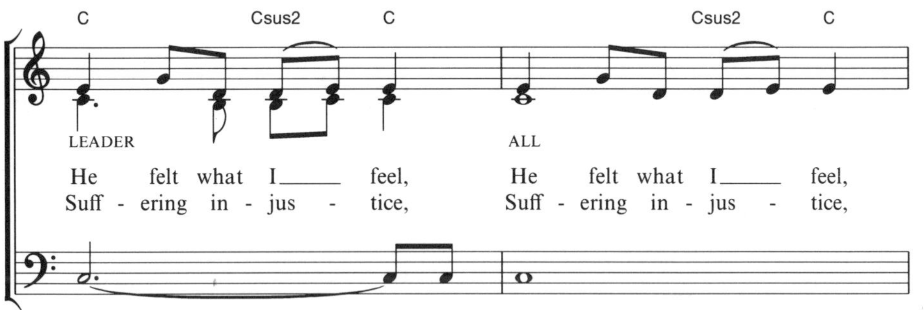
C
Csus2
C
Csus2
C
LEADER
ALL
He felt what I feel, He felt what I feel,
Suff - ering in - jus - tice, Suff - ering in - jus - tice,

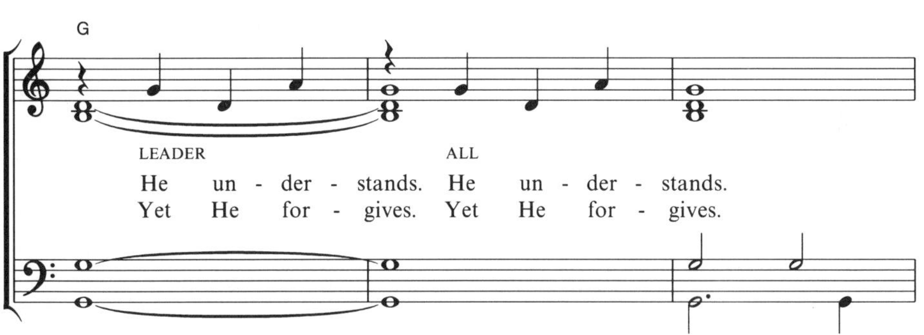
G
LEADER
ALL
He un - der - stands. He un - der - stands.
Yet He for - gives. Yet He for - gives.

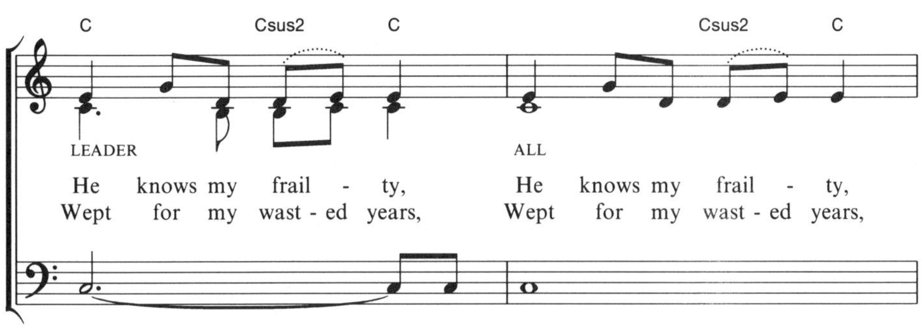
C
Csus2
C
Csus2
C
LEADER
ALL
He knows my frail - ty, He knows my frail - ty,
Wept for my wast - ed years, Wept for my wast - ed years,

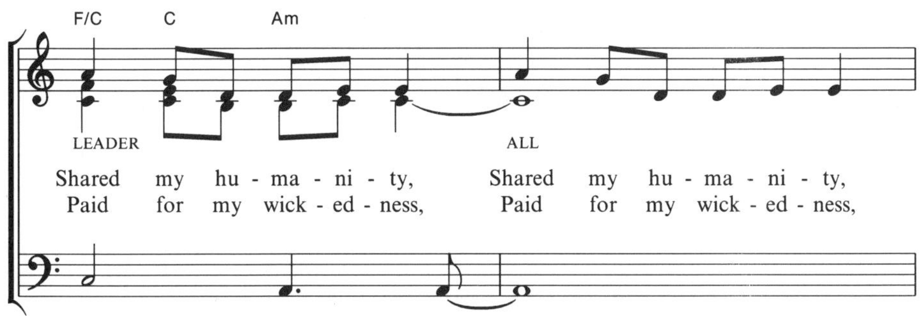
F/C
C
Am
LEADER
ALL
Shared my hu - ma - ni - ty, Shared my hu - ma - ni - ty,
Paid for my wick - ed - ness, Paid for my wick - ed - ness,

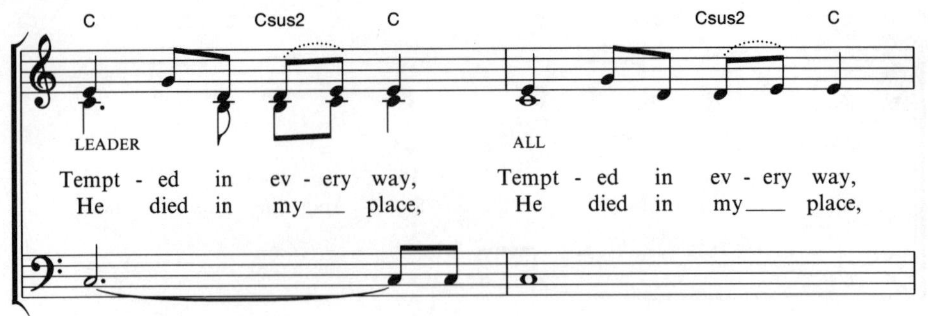
C
Csus2
C
Csus2
C
LEADER
ALL
Tempt - ed in ev - ery way, Tempt - ed in ev - ery way,
He died in my ___ place, He died in my ___ place,

G
LEADER
ALL
Yet with - out sin. Yet with - out sin.
That I might live. That I might live.

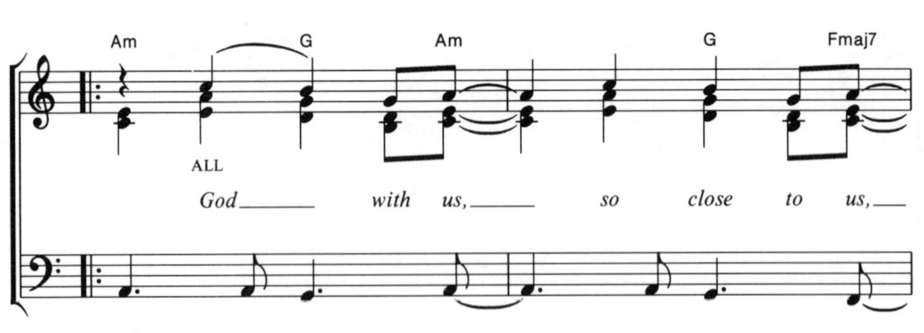
Am
G
Am
G
Fmaj7
ALL
God ___ with us, ___ so close to us, ___

G
Am
G
Fmaj7
Am
Fmaj7
__ God ___ with us, ___ Im - man - u - el! ___

1.3.4.5.
G
2.
To next verse D.C.
6.

1 He walked where I walk,
He stood where I stand,
He felt what I feel,
He understands.
He knows my frailty,
Shared my humanity,
Tempted in every way,
Yet without sin.
God with us, so close to us,
God with us, Immanuel!

2 One of a hated race,
Stung by the prejudice,
Suffering injustice,
Yet He forgives.
Wept for my wasted years,
Paid for my wickedness,
He died in my place,
That I might live.
God with us . . .

679 He who dwells

Words and Music
Chris A Bowater

Women: First time
Men: Repeat
B♭9
Cm7
He___ who dwells,
He___ who dwells_ in the
B♭9
Cm7
Women: First time
Men: Repeat
E♭maj7
Dm
shel-ter of___ the most high (will) rest in the sha-dow,_ the
E♭maj7
1.
Dm7
2.
F7
ALL
MEN
sha-dow of___ the Al-migh-ty___ (will) migh-ty. And I'll
B♭
B♭/A
Gm
Dm/F
E♭
E♭
E♭/D
Cm7
say of the Lord He is__ my re-fuge.________ And I'll say of the

F
F7
B♭9
Cm7
B♭
B♭/A
Lord He is my strength. And I'll make of the
Gm
Dm/F
E♭
E♭/D
Cm7
Fsus
F
most High one my dwell-ing place. And I'll say He is my God, I'll
D
Gm
Cm7
F7
B♭
say He is my God, I will say He is my God in whom I trust.

WOMEN
He who dwells, He who dwells
In the shelter of the most high,
MEN
He who dwells, He who dwells
In the shelter of the most high will
WOMEN
Rest in the shadow,
The shadow of the Almighty,
MEN
Will rest in the shadow,
The shadow of the Almighty.
ALL
And I'll say of the Lord He is my refuge.
And I'll say of the Lord He is my strength.
And I'll make of the most High one my dwelling-place.
And I'll say He is my God,
I'll say He is my God,
I will say He is my God in whom I trust.

680 Holy Spirit, we welcome You

Words and music
Chris Bowater

Prayerfully
Capo 3(A)
C
(A)
Dm/C
(Bm)
Cmaj7
(Amaj7)
Ho - ly Spi - rit, we wel - come You,
1.
2.
Csus
(Asus)
B♭/C
(G)
C7
(A7)
Fmaj7
(Dmaj7)
Move a - mong
G/F
(F)
Em7
(C♯m7)
Am7
(F♯m7)
us with ho - ly fire
Dm7
(Bm7)
G7
(E7)
Cmaj7
(Amaj7)
C7sus
(A7sus)
As we lay a - side all earth - ly de - sire,

C7
(A7)
Fmaj7
(Dmaj7)
G/F
(E)
Hands reach out and our
Em7
(C#m7)
Am7
(F#m7)
F
(D)
hearts as - pire. Ho - ly Spi - rit,
C
(A)
Dm7
(Bm7)
Ho-ly Spi - rit, Ho-ly Spi - rit,
1.2.
3.
F/G
(D)
G7sus
(E7sus)
C
(A)
Dm/C
(Bm)
C
(A)
we wel-come You!

2 Holy Spirit, we welcome You,
Holy Spirit, we welcome You!
Let the breeze of Your presence blow
That Your children here might truly know
How to move in the Spirit's flow.
Holy Spirit, Holy Spirit,
Holy Spirit, we welcome You!

3 Holy Spirit, we welcome You,
Holy Spirit, we welcome You!
Please accomplish in us today
Some new work of loving grace, we pray –
Unreservedly – have Your way.
Holy Spirit, Holy Spirit,
Holy Spirit, we welcome You!

681 Holy is the Lord

Words and music
Kelly Green

Majestically
Men and women in canon
Em
Cmaj7
WOMEN: Ho - ly is the *etc.*
MEN: Ho - ly is the Lord.
Ho - ly is the Lord.
Ho - ly is the
Lord.
Ho - ly is the Lord.
Right-eous-ness and mer - cy,
Judge-ment and

Em
Cmaj7
Em
Cmaj7
Em
Cmaj7
grace. Faith-ful-ness and sov-ereign-ty;

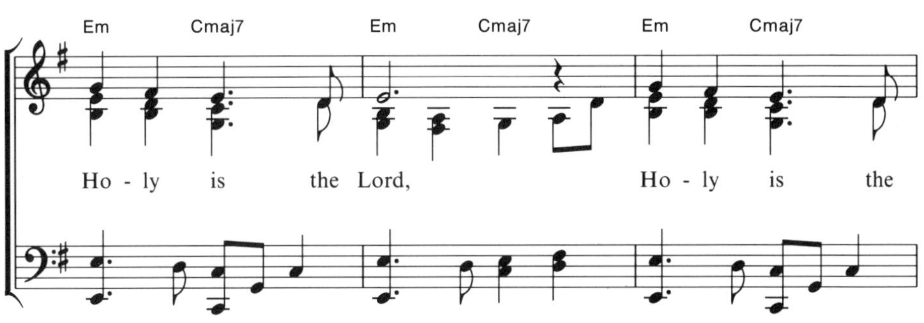
Em
Cmaj7
Em
Cmaj7
Em
Cmaj7
Ho - ly is the Lord, Ho - ly is the

1.
2.
Em
Cmaj7
Em
Cmaj7
E
Lord. Lord.

MEN AND WOMEN IN CANON

Holy is the Lord.
Holy is the Lord.
Holy is the Lord.
Holy is the Lord.
Righteousness and mercy,
Judgement and grace.
Faithfulness and sovereignty;
Holy is the Lord,
Holy is the Lord.

682 Hosanna, hosanna

Words and music
Carl Tuttle

Lively
G
D
Em
C
1 Ho - san - na, ho - san - na, ho - san-na in the high -
2 Glo - ry, glo - ry, glo-ry to the King of
D
G
D
- est, Ho - san - na, ho - san - na, ho -
kings; Glo - ry, glo - ry,
Em
C
D
C
D
- san-na in the high - est,
glo-ry to the King of kings;
Lord, we lift up Your name,
G
C
D
G
with hearts full of praise.

C
D
G
D
Em
Be ex - alt - ed, O___ Lord my God – Ho -
1.
2.
C
D
G
- san - na, in the high - est.
glo - ry to the King of kings.

1 Hosanna, hosanna, hosanna in the highest,
Hosanna, hosanna, hosanna in the highest,
Lord, we lift up Your name, with hearts full of praise.
Be exalted, O Lord my God – Hosanna, in the highest.

2 Glory, glory, glory to the King of kings;
Glory, glory, glory to the King of kings;
Lord, we lift up Your name, with hearts full of praise.
Be exalted, O Lord my God – glory to the King of kings.

683 Holy child

Words: Timothy Dudley-Smith
Music: Michael Baughen
arranged Phil Burt

Tenderly
G
C
Am
1 Ho-ly child, how still You lie! Safe the man-ger, soft the
D
G
G7
C
hay; Faint up - on the east-ern sky Breaks the
G
D
G
Fine
C
dawn of Christ - mas Day.
2 Ho - ly child, whose birth-day
Am
D7
G
B7
Em
brings Shep-herds from their field and fold, An-gel

Am
E7
Am
D
A7
D
choirs and east-ern kings, Myrrh and frank - in-cense and gold:

1 Holy child, how still You lie!
Safe the manger, soft the hay;
Faint upon the eastern sky
Breaks the dawn of Christmas Day.

2 Holy child, whose birthday brings
Shepherds from their field and fold,
Angel choirs and eastern kings,
Myrrh and frankincense and gold:

3 Holy child, what gift of grace
From the Father freely willed!
In Your infant form we trace
All God's promises fulfilled.

4 Holy child, whose human years
Span like ours delight and pain;
One in human joys and tears,
One in all but sin and stain:

5 Holy child, so far from home,
All the lost to seek and save:
To what dreadful death You come,
To what dark and silent grave!

6 Holy child, before whose Name
Powers of darkness faint and fall;
Conquered death and sin and shame –
Jesus Christ is Lord of all!

7 Holy child, how still You lie!
Safe the manger, soft the hay;
Clear upon the eastern sky
Breaks the dawn of Christmas Day.

684 He was pierced

(Like a lamb)

Words and music
Maggi Dawn

Thoughtfully
D A/D G D/F♯ D/G A
1 He was pierced for our trans - gres - sions,
(2) led like a lamb to the slaugh-ter,
D/F♯ G D/F♯ A D
And bruised for our in - i - qui - ties;
Al - though He was in - no - cent of crime;
A/D G D/F♯ D/G
And to bring us peace He was
And cut off from the land of the
A D/F♯ G D/F♯
pun - ished,
liv - ing,
And by His
He paid for the guilt

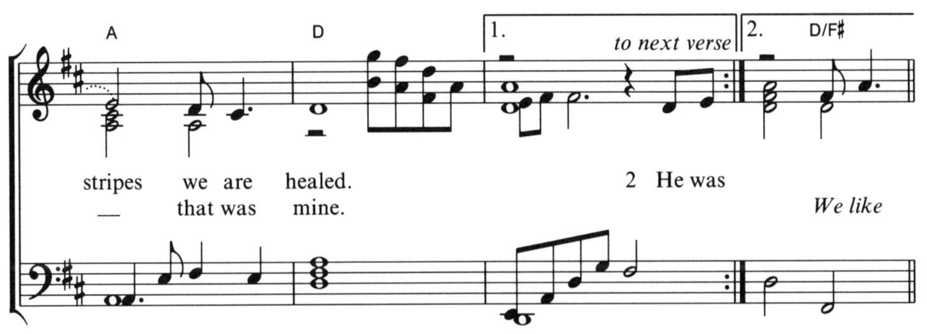
A
D
1.
to next verse
2.
D/F♯
stripes we are healed.
— that was mine.
2 He was
We like

Descant – on repeat only
G D/F♯ Em Em/D A D/F♯
lamb, like a lamb, to the
sheep have gone a - stray, Turned each

G D/F♯ Em Em/D A D/F♯
slaugh - ter He came, And the
one to his own way, And the

G
D/F♯
Em
Em/D
A
Lord laid on Him The in -
Lord has laid on Him The in -
G
D/F♯
D/G
A
D
Dsus
1.
D
2.
D
- i - qui - ty of us all. Like a
- i - qui - ty of us all. We like

1 He was pierced for our transgressions,
And bruised for our iniquities;
And to bring us peace He was punished,
And by His stripes we are healed.

2 He was led like a lamb to the slaughter,
Although He was innocent of crime;
And cut off from the land of the living,
He paid for the guilt that was mine.
We like sheep have gone astray,
Turned each one to his own way,
And the Lord has laid on Him
The iniquity of us all.
We like sheep . . .

685 How lovely is Thy dwelling-place

Psalm 84

Author unknown
Music arranged Phil Burt

Capo 3(D)
B♭/C (G/A) F (D) B♭ (G) F (D) Gm (Em) F (D)
How love-ly is Thy dwell-ing-place, O Lord of
Dm (Bm) F (D) Gm7 (Em7)
hosts, My soul longs and yearns for Your courts,
Gm7/C (Em7/A) C7 (A7) F (D) Gm (Em) C7 (A7) B♭/C (G/A) F (D)
And my heart and flesh sing for joy to the liv-ing God.
B♭/C (G/A) F (D) B♭ (G) F (D) Gm (Em) F (D)
One day in Thy pres - ence is far bet-ter to me than

Dm
(Bm)
F
(D)
Gm
(Em)
gold, Or to live my whole life some-where
Gm7
(Em7)
Gm7/C
(Em7/A)
C7
(A7)
F
(D)
else, And I would ra - ther
B♭ F Gm
(G) (D) (Em)
F
(D)
A7/C♯
(F♯/A♯)
Dm7
(Bm7)
B♭/C
(G/A)
be a door - keep-er in Your house Than to
F
(D)
Gm
(Em)
Gm7
(Em7)
take my fate up-on my - self.

Gm/C
(Em/A)
C7
(A7)
F
(D)
B♭
(G)
F
(D)
Gm
(Em)
You are my sun and my shield, You are my
F
(D)
A7
(F♯)
Dm
(Bm)
C7
(A7)
F
(D)
B♭
(G)
F
(D)
lov-er from the start, And the high-way to Your
Gm
(Em)
C7
(A7)
F
(D)
B♭
(G)
F
(D)
ci - ty runs through my heart.

How lovely is Thy dwelling-place, O Lord of hosts,
My soul longs and yearns for Your courts,
And my heart and flesh sing for joy to the living God.
One day in Thy presence is far better to me than gold,
Or to live my whole life somewhere else,
And I would rather be a door-keeper in Your house
Than to take my fate upon myself.
You are my sun and my shield,
You are my lover from the start,
And the highway to Your city runs through my heart.

686 I am the Bread

Words and music
Brian Hoare

D/F♯ G A7/G F♯m7 Bm7
1 I am the Bread, The Bread of Life; Who comes to
(2) Vine, The liv - ing Vine; A - part from
(3) bread, and drink this wine, and as you
Em7 A Dmaj7 D/F♯ G A7/G
me will ne - ver hun - ger. I am the Bread, The Bread of
me you can do no - thing. I am the Vine, The re - al
do, re-ceive this life of mine. All that I am I give to
F♯m7 Bm7 Em7 A 1.2. D D7 3. D Fine
heaven; Who feeds on me will ne - ver die. And as you
Vine: A - bide in me and I in you. And as you
you, that you may live for ev - er - more.
G A7/G F♯m7 Bm7
eat, re - mem - ber me — my bo - dy
drink, re - mem - ber me — my blood was

Em7
A7
D
D7
G
A7/G
bro - ken on the tree: my life was given to set you
shed up-on the tree: my life was given to set you

F♯m7
Bm7
Esus
E
A
A7/G
A7/F♯
free, and I'm a - live for ev - er - more. 2 I am the
free, and I'm a - live for ev - er - more. 3 So eat this

1 I am the Bread,
The Bread of Life;
Who comes to me will never hunger.
I am the Bread,
The Bread of heaven;
Who feeds on me will never die.
And as you eat, remember me –
My body broken on the tree:
My life was given to set you free,
And I'm alive for evermore.

2 I am the Vine,
The living Vine;
Apart from me you can do nothing.
I am the Vine,
The real Vine:
Abide in me and I in you.
And as you drink, remember me –
My blood was shed upon the tree:
My life was given to set you free,
And I'm alive for evermore.

3 So eat this bread,
And drink this wine,
And as you do, receive this life of mine.
All that I am I give to you,
That you may live for evermore.

687 I am a wounded soldier

Words and music
Danny Daniels

Gospel feel
Capo 3(C)
F (D)
B♭/F (G/D)
B♭6/F (G6/D)
Dm (Bm)
C (A)
B♭/C (G/A)
I am a wound-ed sold - ier _ but I
will not leave the fight, _ Be - cause the Great Phy-si - cian is
heal - ing _ me. _ So I'm _ stand-ing in the bat - tle, _ in the

F (D) Dm (Bm) C (A)
armour of His light, Because His mighty power is
F (D) B♭/F (G/D) F (D) Gm7 (Em7) B♭ (G) F (D)
real in me. I am loved, I am accepted by the
C (A) F/C (D/A) C (A) B♭ (G) F (D) B♭ (G)
Saviour of my soul. I am loved, I am accept-
F (D) A7 (F♯7) Dm (Bm) F/C (D/A) Gm7/C (Em7/A) 1. F (D) B♭/F (G/D)
-ed and my wounds will be made whole.

2.
B♭
(G)
F/A
(D/F♯)
Dm
(Bm)
F/C
(D/A)
B♭6/C
(G6/A)
Dm
(Bm)
Dm/C
(Bm/A)
G7/B
(E7/G♯)
whole, and my wounds will be made whole and my
F/C
(D/A)
B♭6/C
(G6/A)
F
(D)
B♭/F
(G/D)
wounds will be made whole.
F
(D)
B♭6/C
(G6/D)
F
(D)
B♭6/C
(G6/D)
F
(D)

I am a wounded soldier but I will not leave the fight,
Because the Great Physician is healing me.
So I'm standing in the battle, in the armour of His light,
Because His mighty power is real in me.
I am loved, I am accepted by the Saviour of my soul.
I am loved, I am accepted and my wounds will be made whole.

688 I believe in Jesus

Words and music
Marc Nelson

♩ = 82
E
A
A/C♯
B/D♯
Build 2nd and 3rd times
E
A
Bsus
B7
1 I___ be-lieve in Je - sus_
2 and 3 I___ be-lieve in You, Lord,
E
A
B7
I be-lieve He is the Son of God.
I be-lieve You are the Son of God;
E
A
Bsus
B7
I be-lieve He died and rose a - gain,
I be-lieve You died and rose a - gain:

E A B7 A B/D♯
I be-lieve He paid for us all. And I be-lieve He's
I be-lieve You paid for us all: MEN: And I be-lieve You're
E E/G♯ A B7 E
WOMEN: I be-lieve that You're here.
here now Stand-ing in our midst
here now, ALL: Stand-ing in our midst.
A B/D♯ E E/G♯
With the pow - er to
Here with the pow - er to heal now
MEN: Here with the pow - er to heal now,
A B7 1. E B/E 2. E A/C♯ B/D♯
heal,
And the grace to for - give.
ALL: And the grace to for - give.

3.
E
E/G♯
A
B/D♯
E
E/G♯
- give.
And I
be-lieve
He's
here
now
A
B
E
A
B
Stand-ing
in our
midst
Here with the pow - er to heal
E
E/G♯
rit.
A
B
E
now
And the grace
to for - give.

1 I believe in Jesus
I believe He is the Son of God.
I believe He died and rose again,
I believe He paid for us all.
And I believe He's here now
Standing in our midst
Here with the power to heal now
And the grace to forgive.

2 I believe in You, Lord,
I believe You are the Son of God;
I believe You died and rose again:
I believe You paid for us all:
MEN And I believe You're here now,
WOMEN I believe that You're here.
ALL Standing in our midst.
MEN Here with the power to heal now,
WOMEN With the power to heal,
ALL And the grace to forgive.

3 I believe in You, Lord . . . (All verse 2)
And I believe He's here now . . . (2nd half of verse 1)

689 I look to the hills

Psalm 121

Words and Music
Greg Leavers
arranged Phil Burt

Majestically
D
Am
D7
G
G/F♯
I look to the hills From where shall my help
Em
A
Dmaj
Bm
3
Em
A
3
come; My help comes from the Lord, Ma - ker of
Em
A7
D
Fine
Em7
(v2.)
F♯m
Bm7
Heaven and Earth. He will not al -
Asus4
A7
A7/G
F♯
Bm7
Asus
A7/G
- low Your_ foot to ev - er slip

D/F♯
D7/F♯
G9
Gm/B♭
(v3.)
D/A
E/G♯
Asus
A7
He who keeps you will not sleep. I

I look to the hills
From where shall my help come;
My help comes from the Lord,
Maker of Heaven and Earth.

1 He will not allow
Your foot to ever slip
He who keeps you will not sleep.
I look to the hills . . .

2 He watches over you
As your shade from moon and sun
He will keep you from all harm.
I look to the hills . . .

3 He will guard your ways
As you come and as you go
From this time and forever more.
I look to the hills . . .

690 I rest in God alone

Words and music: John Daniels
Music arranged Christopher Norton

Steadily
Capo 3(D) F (D) C/B♭ (A/G) Cm/E♭ (Am/C) D7 (B7)
Gm (Em) C (A) F (D) B♭/F (G/D)
F (D) Am (F♯m) Dm (Bm) Am (F♯m) B♭ (G)
I rest in God a - lone, From Him comes
Gm7 (Em7) F/C (D/A) B♭/C (G/A) C7 (A7) F (D)
my sal - va - tion; My soul finds
Am (F♯m) Dm (Bm) Am (F♯m) B♭ (G)
rest in Him, My for - tress –

Gm7
(Em7)
F/C
(D/A)
C
(A)
B♭/C
(G/A)
C
(A)
F/A
(D/F♯)
I'll not be sha - ken.
1 My hope is in
2 O trust in Him,
B♭
(G)
C
(A)
A/C♯
(F♯/A♯)
Dm
(Bm)
the Lord My hon-our and strength; My re-fuge is in
you peo - ple, Pour out your hearts, For God is our re -
G
(E)
B♭/C
(G/A)
C7
(A7)
B♭/C
(G/A)
C
(A)
F/A
(D/F♯)
Him for ev - er,
- fuge for ev - er,
My trust and
C/B♭
(A/G)
Cm/E♭
(Am/C)
D7
(B7)
Gm7
(Em7)
all of my heart
In Him a - lone
after verse 2 D.𝄋
1.
to end
B♭/C
(G/A)
F
(D)
B♭/F
(G/D)
F
(D)
B♭/F
(G/D)
F
(D)
my soul finds rest.

691 I love You, O Lord, You alone

Words: Christopher Idle
Music: David Peacock
With assurance
G D7/A G/B C
I love You, O Lord, You a - lone, My
G/D Em7 Am D G D7/A
re - fuge on whom I de - pend; My Ma - ker, my Sav - iour, my
G/B C G/D Em7 Am7 D7 Gsus G
own, My hope and my trust with-out end. The
E♭ A♭ Gm7 C7
Lord is my strength and my song, De -

Fm
Cm
Dsus
D
G
D7/A
- fen - der and Guide of my ways;
My
Mas - ter to whom I be -
G/B
C
G/D
Em7
Am7
D7
Gsus
G
- long,
My
God
who shall have
all
my
praise.

1 I love You, O Lord, You alone,
My refuge on whom I depend;
My Maker, my Saviour, my own,
My hope and my trust without end.
The Lord is my strength and my song,
Defender and Guide of my ways;
My Master to whom I belong,
My God who shall have all my praise.

2 The dangers of death gathered round,
The waves of destruction came near;
But in my despairing I found
The Lord who released me from fear.
I called for His help in my pain,
To God my salvation I cried;
He brought me His comfort again,
I live by the strength He supplied.

3 The earth and the elements shake
With thunder and lightning and hail;
The cliffs and the mountaintops break
And mortals are feeble and pale.
His justice is full and complete,
His mercy to us has no end
The clouds are a path for His feet,
He comes on the wings of the wind.

4 My hope is the promise He gives,
My life is secure in His hand;
I shall not be lost, for He lives!
He comes to my side – I shall stand!
Lord God, You are powerful to save,
Your Spirit will spur me to pray;
Your Son has defeated the grave:
I trust and I praise You today!

692 I cannot count Your blessings

Words and music
Phil Rogers

D Gmaj7 A7 G/D D
I can-not count Your bless-ings, Lord, they're won-der-ful.
Bm7 Em9 A7
I can't be-gin to mea-sure Your great
D D7 Gmaj7 A7
love. I can-not count the times You have for-
D F#7 Bm7 Em7
-giv - en me, And changed me by Your

A7
D
G
D
Spi - rit from a - bove.
Asus
A7
Dmaj7
Gmaj7
How I wor - ship You, my Fa - ther, You are
Dsus
D
Asus
A7
Dmaj7
won - der - ful. How I glo - ri - fy You,
Gmaj7
D
D7
Gmaj7
Je - sus, You're my Lord. How I praise You, Ho - ly

Em9
D
A/C♯
Bm
Spi - rit, You have changed my life, And You're

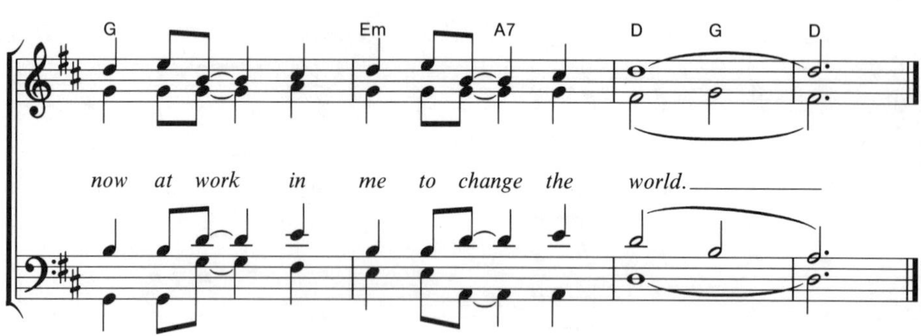
G
Em
A7
D
G
D
now at work in me to change the world.

1 I cannot count Your blessings, Lord, they're wonderful.
I can't begin to measure Your great love.
I cannot count the times You have forgiven me,
And changed me by Your Spirit from above.
How I worship You, my Father, You are wonderful.
How I glorify You, Jesus, You're my Lord.
How I praise You, Holy Spirit, You have changed my life,
And You're now at work in me to change the world.

2 When I was blind You opened up my eyes to see.
When I was dead You gave me life anew.
When I was lost You found me and You rescued me,
And carried me, rejoicing, home with You.
How I worship You . . .

3 I cannot count Your mercies, Lord, they're marvellous.
I can't begin to measure Your great grace.
I cannot count the times that You have answered me,
Whenever I have prayed and sought Your face.
How I worship You . . .

4 Whenever I consider what I am to You,
My heart is filled with wonder, love and awe.
I want to share with others that You love them too,
And tell the world of Jesus, more and more.
How I worship You . . .

693 I see perfection

Children of the King

Words and music: Chris Eaton
Music arranged Christopher Hayward

Flowing
Em
D/E
Em
D
1 I see per - fec - tion as I
2 Your Ho - ly Spi - rit will for
C
G/B
C
Dsus
D
Em
D/E
look in Your eyes, Lord; There's no re -
ev - er con - trol me! I give my
Em
D
C
G/B
C
Dsus
D
- jec - tion as I look in Your eyes, Lord.
pre - sent, fu - ture, past, to You com - plete - ly.
Animated
Em
G
You are a ri - ver that is ne - ver dry,

Em Am7 D C/D D
You are_ the star that lights the eve - ning sky,
Em G
You are_ my God and I__ will fol - low You,
Em Am7 D C/D D
And now I know just where I'm go - ing_ to.__
Triumphantly
G D/G C/G G G D/F♯ Am7 G/C
We are child-ren, child-ren of_ the King We will praise Your
D C/D D C B7
name, Glo - ri - fy_ You, mag - ni - fy_ You

Em
Cm6
G/D
C/D
G/D
Je - sus, we can ne-ver de - ny Your love for us

C/D
G/D
C/D
Am/D
G
D/G
C/G
G/D
on the cross
Now You've made us child-ren of the King.

1.
C
Am7
Dsus
D
2.
C/D
Am/D
G
D/G
G
Now You've made us child-ren of the King.

1 I see perfection as I look in Your eyes, Lord;
There's no rejection as I look in Your eyes, Lord.
You are a river that is never dry,
You are the star that lights the evening sky,
You are my God and I will follow You,
And now I know just where I'm going to.
We are children, children of the King
We will praise Your name,
Glorify You, magnify You
Jesus, we can never deny
Your love for us on the cross
Now You've made us children of the King.

2 Your Holy Spirit will for ever control me!
I give my present, future, past, to You completely.
You are a river . . .
We are children . . .
Now You've made us children of the King!

694 I want to thank You

Words and music
Colin Waller
arranged Noël Tredinnick

Bouncy and with life
C
Cmaj7
F
C
F
C
F
Unison or Harmony
I want to thank You, I want to praise You,
Gsus
G
F
C
Dm
C
Cmaj7
F
C
I want to love You more each day.
I want to thank You,
F
C
D
D7
G7
C
Cmaj7

1.2.3.
I want to praise You, Yours is the power, the truth, the way.
C F C C F Gsus G F C Dm
Unison
Fa - ther, Your love I feel; Help me to show it
Ooo etc.
C Cmaj7 Fsus9 F C Fsus9 F C
dolce (gentle)
to be real. Then I can op - en-ly say,
D D7 G7 C Cmaj7 Fsus9 F C

Yours is the power, the truth, the way.
4.
truth, the way.
F C F Gsus G F C Dm Gsus G G D Em
(bouncy)
Descant
I want to thank You, I want to praise and to love You
Unison
I want to thank You, I want to praise You, I want to love You
D G D G D
more each day.
I want to
more each day.
I want to thank You,
E A7 D

thank You, I want to praise with Your pow - er,
I want to praise You, Yours is the pow - er,
G D G D G D
Yours is the power, the truth, the way.
Yours is the power, the truth, the way.
G D Asus A7 D Dmaj7
G D G D G Asus A7 D

I want to thank You, I want to praise You,
I want to love You more each day.
I want to thank You, I want to praise You,
Yours is the power, the truth, the way.

1 Father, Your love I feel;
Help me to show it to be real.
Then I can openly say,
Yours is the power, the truth, the way.
I want to thank You . . .

2 Jesus, Your Word I hear;
Help me to see its truth so clear.
So I can openly say,
Yours is the power, the truth, the way.
I want to thank You . . .

3 Spirit, Your power I know;
Help me to feel it, and to grow
Stronger in every way, – 'cause
Yours is the power, the truth, the way.
I want to thank You . . . (twice)

695 I will build my church

Words and music
Graham Kendrick

Brightly
G C G C G C G G
MEN: 'I will build my church, And the
WOMEN: I will build my church,
Em D
gates of hell, Shall not pre - vail, A -
And the gates of hell, Shall not pre-vail, A -
1. 2.
Cmaj7 Dsus D Cmaj7 Dsus D G C D
ALL MEN ALL
- gainst ___ it.' I will - gainst ___ it.' So you
G Em C D G Em
powers in the hea-vens a-bove, Bow down! And you powers on the earth be-low,

C Am D
C D
B7 Em
Bow down! And ac - know - ledge that Je - sus,
C D
B7/D♯ Em
Am7
Je - sus, Je - sus is Lord,
D
G C G C
to repeat
G C G
last time
G C G
Is Lord!
MEN: I will

MEN	'I will build my church,
WOMEN	I will build my church,
MEN	And the gates of hell,
WOMEN	And the gates of hell,
MEN	Shall not prevail,
WOMEN	Shall not prevail,
ALL	Against it.'
MEN	I will build . . .

ALL *So you powers in the heavens above,*
Bow down!
And you powers on the earth below,
Bow down!
And acknowledge that Jesus,
Jesus, Jesus is Lord,
Is Lord!

696 I will give You praise

Words and music
Tommy Walker

D
Em7
I will give You praise, I will sing Your song, I will

D
G
D
bless Your ho - ly Name; For there is no o-ther God Who is

Em
D
G
like un-to You, You're the on - ly way, On-ly You

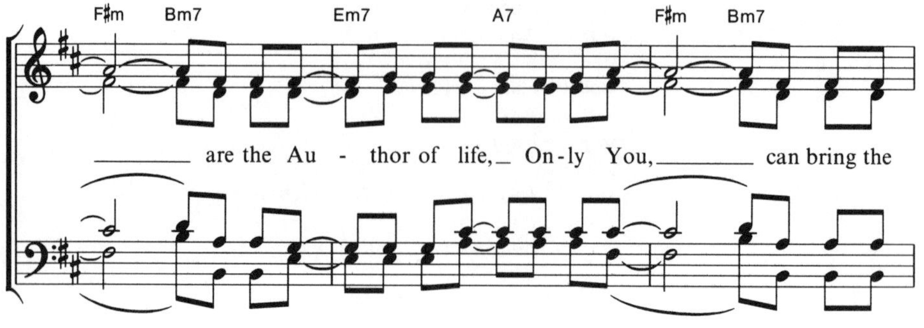
F♯m
Bm7
Em7
A7
F♯m
Bm7
are the Au - thor of life, On-ly You, can bring the

Em7
A7
F♯m
Bm7
blind their sight, On - ly You, are called
Em7
A7
F♯m7
Bm7
Em7
A7
Prince of Peace, On-ly You pro-mised You'd ne-ver leave.
G
F♯m
Em7
A7
D
On - ly You are God.

I will give You praise,
I will sing Your song,
I will bless Your holy Name;
For there is no other God
Who is like unto You,
You're the only way,
Only You are the Author of life,
Only You, can bring the blind their sight,
Only You, are called Prince of Peace,
Only You promised You'd never leave.
Only You are God.

697 If my people

Words and music
Graham Kendrick

Gently
Capo 4(Am)
C♯m (Am)
B (G)
C♯m (Am)
B (G)
C♯m (Am)
B (G)
If my peo - ple who
C♯m (Am)
B (G)
Amaj7 (Fmaj7)
A6 (F6)
bear my name, Will hum - ble them-selves and
E (C)
C♯m (Am)
B (G)
C♯m (Am)
B (G)
pray; If they seek my pres - ence And turn their
Amaj7 (Fmaj7)
A6 (F6)
G♯sus (Esus)
G♯7
backs on their wick - ed ways;

C#7
(A7)
F#m
(Dm)
B7
(G7)
E
(C)
Then I will hear from hea - ven, I'll hear from
F#m
(Dm)
C#m
(Am)
G#sus
(Esus)
G#7
(E7)
C#7
(A7)
F#m
(Dm)
hea - ven and will for - give. I will for-give their
B7
(G7)
E
(C)
F#m
(Dm)
C#m
(Am)
sins And will heal their land – Yes I will
F#m6
(Dm)
G#
(E)
C#m
(Am)
to end
heal their land.

If my people who bear my name,
Will humble themselves and pray;
If they seek my presence
And turn their backs on their wicked ways;
Then I will hear from heaven,
I'll hear from heaven and will forgive.
I will forgive their sins
And will heal their land –
Yes I will heal their land.

698 I'm accepted

Words and music
Rob Hayward

Worshipfully
Capo 4(C)
E (C) A (F) E (C) A (F)
I'm ac-cept - ed, I'm for-giv - en, I am
E (C) A (F) B7 (G)
fa-thered by the true_ and liv-ing God._ I'm ac-cept-
E (C) A (F) E (C) A (F)
- ed, no con-dem-na - tion, I am
E (C) A (F) B7 (G) E (C) E7 (C7)
loved by the true and liv-ing God. There's no

A
(F)
B7
(G)
G♯m
(Em)
C♯m
(Am)
guilt or fear as I draw near To the
A
(F)
B7
(G)
E
(C)
A
(F)
B7
(G)
Sav-iour and Cre-a-tor of the world. There is joy and peace as
G♯m
(Em)
C♯m
(Am)
A
(F)
B7
(G)
E
(C)
I re - lease My wor - ship to You, O Lord.

I'm accepted, I'm forgiven,
I am fathered by the true and living God.
I'm accepted, no condemnation,
I am loved by the true and living God.
There's no guilt or fear as I draw near
To the Saviour and Creator of the world.
There is joy and peace as I release
My worship to You, O Lord.

699 Immanuel, O Immanuel

Words and music
Graham Kendrick

Worshipfully, but with strength

Em7 G/A A

Im -

A/D D Asus A A/D D A/C♯

- man - u - el, O Im - man - u - el, Bowed in

Bm E9 Em7 A

awe I wor-ship at Your feet, And sing Im -

A/D D Asus A Dsus2 Bsus B
3
- man - u - el, God is with us, Shar-ing my

Gmaj7 A/G F#m7 Bm7
hu-man-ness, my shame, Feel-ing my weak-ness-es, my pain, Tak-ing the
Csus2 A A/D D A/B B7
pun-ish-ment, the blame, Im - man - u - el. And now my
Gmaj7 A/G F#m7 Bm7
words can-not ex - plain, All that my heart can-not con - tain, How great are the
Csus2 A
glo - ries of Your Name. Im -
G6 A9 D Bm7
- man - - - u - el. Im -

B/E
E
Bsus
B
B/E
E
B/D♯
-man - u - el,
O Im - man - u - el,
Bowed in
C♯m
F♯9
F♯m7
B
awe
I
wor-ship at
Your
feet,
And sing Im -
B/E
E
Bsus
B
Esus2
C♯sus
C♯
3
-man - u - el,
God is
with
us,
Shar-ing my
Amaj7
B/A
3
G♯m7
C♯m7
3
hu-man-ness, my shame, Feel-ing my weak-ness-es, my pain, Tak-ing the
Dsus2
B
B/E
E
B/C♯
C♯7
3
pun-ish-ment, the blame,
Im - man - u - el.
And now my
3

Amaj7
B/A
G♯m7
C♯m7
3
3
words can-not ex - plain, All that my heart can-not con - tain, How great are the

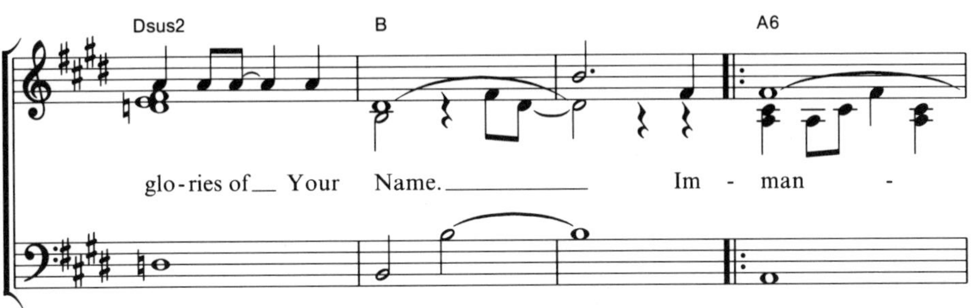
Dsus2
B
A6
glo - ries of __ Your Name. __ Im - man -

B9
E
Esus
1.2.3.
E
4.
E
- u - el. Im - __

Immanuel, O Immanuel,
Bowed in awe I worship at Your feet,
And sing Immanuel, God is with us,
Sharing my humanness, my shame,
Feeling my weaknesses, my pain,
Taking the punishment, the blame,
Immanuel.
And now my words cannot explain,
All that my heart cannot contain,
How great are the glories of Your Name.
Immanuel.

700 I want to serve You, Lord

Words and music
Chris Rolinson

Slowly and steadily with strength
D E F♯m F♯m/E A/C♯ E7sus E7
I want to serve You, Lord, in to - tal a - ban - don -
A D Amaj7/C♯ Bm7 B7 E
- ment, I want to yield my heart to You;
C♯sus C♯7 F♯m E A C♯sus/G♯ C♯7sus C♯7
I want to give my life in all sur - ren -
D+9 D Bm7 E7sus E7 A D/A A
- der, I want to live for You a - lone.

1 I want to serve You, Lord,
in total abandonment,
I want to yield my heart to You;
I want to give my life in all surrender,
I want to live for You alone.

2 I want to give my all
in total abandonment,
Releasing all within my grasp;
I want to live my life in all its fulness,
I want to worship Christ alone.

3 I want to come to You
in total abandonment –
Lord, will You set my heart ablaze?
I want to love You with all my soul and strength,
I want to give You all my days.

701 It's Your blood

Words and music
Michael Christ

Steadily
Capo 3(G)
Cm7/F (Am7/D) E♭/F (C/D) B♭ (G) F/A (D/F♯) Gm7 (Em7) Gm7/F (Em7/D)
It's Your blood that clean - ses_ me, It's Your
E♭ (C) F (D) E♭/F (C/D) E♭ (C) F (D)
blood that gives me life, It's Your blood that took my place In re -
B♭ (G) Dm7 (Bm7) Gm (Em) Gm7/F (Em/D) E♭ (C) E♭m (Cm) E♭m/C (Cm/A)
- deem-ing sac - ri - fice,___ And wash-es me___ whit-er than the
B♭ (G) F/A (D/F♯) Gm7 (Em7) Gm7/F (Em7/D) Cm (Am) E♭/F (C/D) F7 (D7) B♭ (G)
snow,___ than the snow. My Je-sus, God's pre-cious sac - ri - fice.

702 I will magnify

Words and music
Scott Palazzo

Capo 3(G)
B♭
(G)
Cm7
(Am7)
F
(D)
3
I will mag - ni - fy Thy Name a-bove all the
E♭/F
(C/D)
earth; I will mag - ni - fy Thy
1.
B♭/F
(G/D)
Name a-bove all the earth.
2.3.
D7
(B7)
Gm
(Em)
earth. I will sing un - to Thee

F (D)
B♭ (G)
D7 (B7)
Gm (Em)
3
the prais - es in my heart;
I will sing
Cm7 (Am7)
F (D)
to continue
B♭ (G)
un - to Thee
the prais - es in my heart.
E♭ (C)
E♭/F (C/D)
D.C.
last time
B♭ (G)
B♭ (G)
heart.

I will magnify Thy Name above all the earth;
I will magnify Thy Name above all the earth.
I will sing unto Thee the praises in my heart;
I will sing unto Thee the praises in my heart.

703 I want to see Your face

Words and music
Ruth Hooke

Prayerfully
F♯m
F♯m7
Bm7
I want to see Your face, I want to
Em
G9/D
A/C♯
see Your face,
D
F♯m/C♯
Bm
Em
Give You the wor - ship of my heart, of my
Asus
A
D
A/C♯
G/B
Gm/B♭
heart. Giv-ing up my life to You.

D/A
8va
G9/A
8va
Know-ing You (know-ing You),
Lov - ing You (lov - ing You),

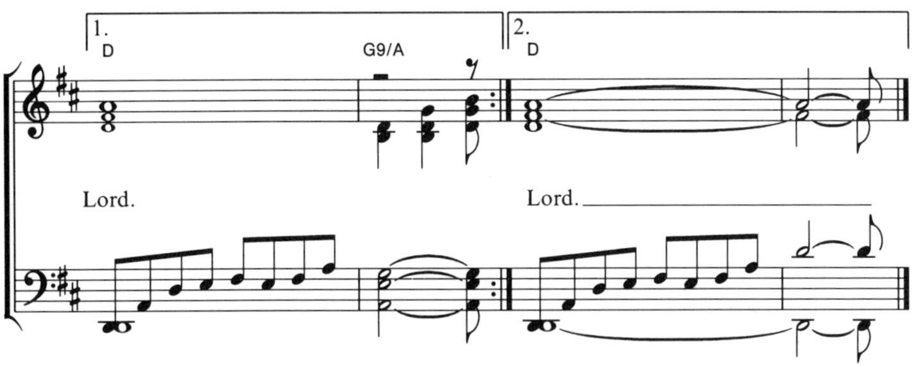
1.
D
G9/A
2.
D
Lord.
Lord.

I want to see Your face,
I want to see Your face,
Give You the worship of my heart, of my heart
Giving up my life to You.
Knowing You (knowing You),
Loving You (loving You), Lord.

704 Jesus I love You

Words and music
Trish Morgan

Gently
Capo 3(D) F (D) B♭/F (G/D) Gm7 (Em7) F (D) B♭/F (G/D) C (A)
8va
mine!)
C7/F (A7/D) F (D) Dm (Bm) Gm7 (Em7)
Je - sus, I love You, Love You more and
C7 (A7) C/F (A/D) F (D) Dm (Bm)
more each day; Je - sus, I love You, Your
Gm7 (Em7) C7 (A7) B♭6 (G6) A7♭9 (F♯7)
3
gent-le touch re - news my heart. It's real - ly no

C/D (A/B)
Dm7 (Bm7)
Gm (Em)
C7 (A7)
won - der why No o - ther love can sat - is - fy,

C/F (A/D)
F (D)
Dm (Bm)
Gm (Em)
C7 (A7)
Je - sus, I love You, You've won this heart of
F (D)
B♭/F (G/D)
C7/F (A7/D)
F (D)
8va
B♭/F (G/D)
Gm7 (Em7)
F (D)
mine!

Jesus, I love You,
Love You more and more each day;
Jesus, I love You,
Your gentle touch renews my heart.
It's really no wonder why
No other love can satisfy,
Jesus, I love You,
You've won this heart of mine!

705 Jesus shall take the highest honour

Words and Music
Chris A Bowater

Bbmaj9
Cm7
Dm7
Ab/Bb
Bb7
Je - sus shall take the high - est hon - our,

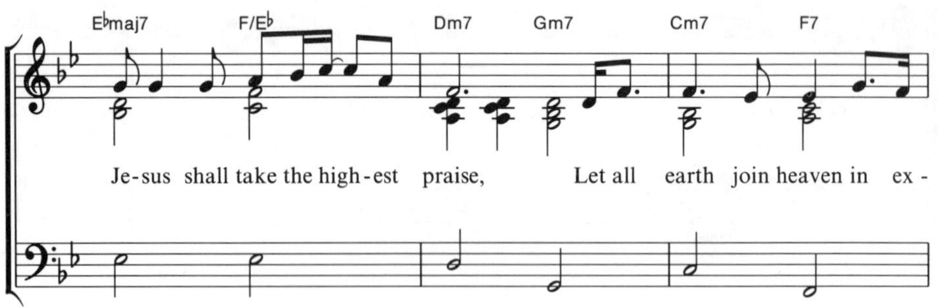
Ebmaj7
F/Eb
Dm7
Gm7
Cm7
F7
Je-sus shall take the high-est praise, Let all earth join heaven in ex -

Bb
Gm7
Ebmaj7
C7/E♮
- alt - ing The Name which is a - bove all o - ther

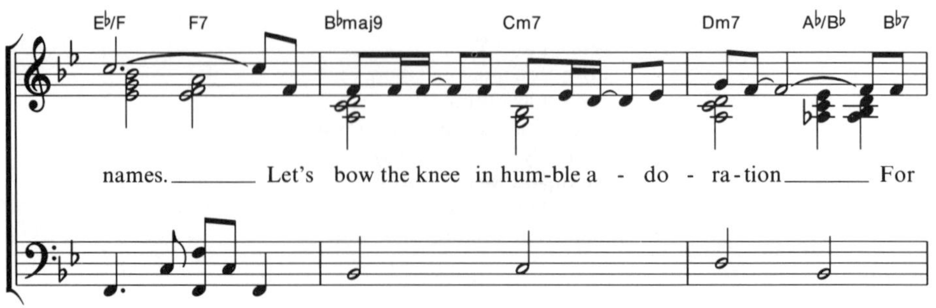
Eb/F
F7
Bbmaj9
Cm7
Dm7
Ab/Bb
Bb7
names. Let's bow the knee in hum-ble a - do - ra - tion For

E♭maj7
F/E♭
Dm7
Gm7
Cm7
F7
at His name ev-ery knee must bow, Let ev-ery tongue con-fess He is
B♭maj7
Gm
E♭maj7
C7/E♮
Christ, God's on - ly Son. Sov-ereign Lord we give you glo - ry
E♭/F
F7
B♭
F/A
Gm
B♭/F
now, For all hon-our and bless-ing and pow-er
E♭
B♭/D
Cm7
Fsus
F
B♭
F/A
Be-longs to You, be-longs to You. All hon-our and bless-ing and

Gm
B♭/F
E♭
B♭/D
Cm7
Fsus
F
pow - er
Be-longs to You,
be-longs to You,
Lord

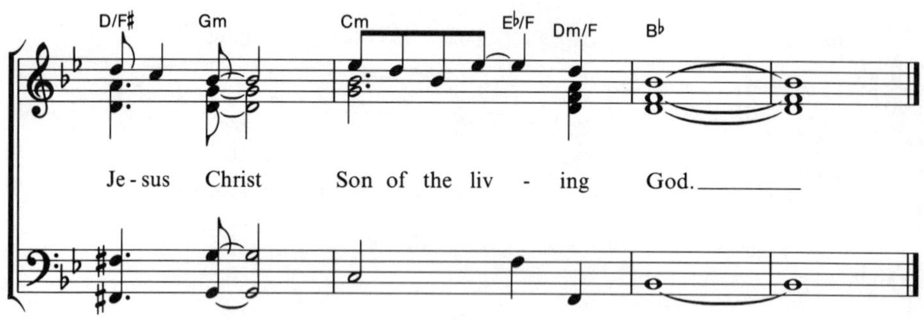
D/F♯
Gm
Cm
E♭/F
Dm/F
B♭
Je - sus Christ
Son of the liv - ing
God.

Jesus shall take the highest honour,
Jesus shall take the highest praise,
Let all earth join heaven in exalting
The Name which is above all other names.
Let's bow the knee in humble adoration
For at His name every knee must bow,
Let every tongue confess He is Christ, God's only Son.
Sovereign Lord we give you glory now,
For all honour and blessing and power
Belongs to You, belongs to You.
All honour and blessing and power
Belongs to You, belongs to You,
Lord Jesus Christ Son of the living God.

706 Jesus Christ our great Redeemer

Words and music
Peter and Diane Fung

Strongly
Capo 2(Am)
Bm (Am) G (F) Bm (Am) G (F)
Je-sus Christ our great Re-deem-er, Migh-ty Vic-tor and strong De-liv-erer,
Dmaj7 (Cmaj7) Em7 (Dm7) A7 (G7) F♯m (Em) Bm (Am) Em (Dm) F♯7 (E7)
King of kings and Lord of lords, We praise You, praise Your name – Al-le -
Bm (Am) A (G) Gmaj7 (Fmaj7) Em (Dm) A7 (G7) Dmaj7 (Cmaj7) F♯7 (E7)
- lu - ia, al-le - lu - ia; King of kings and Lord of lords – Al-le -
Bm (Am) A (G) Gmaj7 (Fmaj7) Em (Dm) A7 (G7) D (C)
- lu - ia, al-le - lu - ia! Your vic-tory is as - sured.

707 Jesus, we celebrate Your victory

Words and music
John Gibson

G D Em D G D Em D
Je - sus, we ce - le-brate Your vic - to - ry,
G D Em D C C D
Je - sus, we re - vel in Your love,
G D Em D G D Em D
Je - sus, we re-joice You've set us free,
G D C D G G7
Je - sus, Your death has brought us life.

C
D
G
D
Em
It was for free - dom that Christ has set us free, No lon -
C
D
C
D
- ger to be sub - ject to a Yoke of sla - ve - ry.
C
D
G
D
Em
So we're re - joic - ing in God's vic - to - ry, Our
C
A7
D
hearts re - spond - ing to His love.

Jesus, we celebrate Your victory,
Jesus, we revel in Your love,
Jesus, we rejoice You've set us free,
Jesus, Your death has brought us life.

1 It was for freedom that Christ has set us free,
No longer to be subject to a Yoke of slavery.
So we're rejoicing in God's victory,
Our hearts responding to His love.
Jesus we celebrate . . .

2 His Spirit in us releases us from fear,
The way to Him is open, with boldness we draw near,
And in His presence our problems disappear,
Our hearts responding to His love.
Jesus we celebrate . . .

708 Joy to the world

Words: I Watts (1674–1748)
Music: G F Handel (1685–1759)
arranged L Mason (1792–1872)

D Em D/A A7 D

1 Joy to the world! The Lord has come: Let
2 Joy to the earth! The Sav - iour reigns: Your
3 He rules the world with truth and grace, And

G A D G/D D

earth re - ceive her King, Let ev - ery heart pre -
sweet - est songs em - ploy, While fields and streams and
makes the na - tions prove The glo - ries of His

G/D
D
- pare Him room And heaven and na - ture sing, And
hills and plains Re - peat the sound-ing joy, Re -
right - eous - ness, The won - ders of His love, The
And heaven and na - ture
Re - peat the sound-ing
The won - ders of His

A
A7
heaven and na - ture sing, And
- peat the sound - ing joy, Re -
won - ders of His love, The
sing, And heaven and na - ture
joy, Re - peat the sound - ing
love, The won - ders of His
D
G/D
D
Em
D/A
A7
D
heaven, and heaven and na - ture sing!
- peat, re - peat the sound - ing joy.
won - ders, won - ders of His love.
sing, And heaven and na - ture sing!
joy, Re - peat the sound - ing joy.
love, The won - ders of His love.

1 Joy to the world! The Lord has come:
Let earth receive her King,
Let every heart prepare Him room
And heaven and nature sing,
And heaven and nature sing,
And heaven, and heaven and nature sing!

2 Joy to the earth! The Saviour reigns:
Your sweetest songs employ
While fields and streams and hills and plains
Repeat the sounding joy,
Repeat the sounding joy,
Repeat, repeat the sounding joy.

3 He rules the world with truth and grace,
And makes the nations prove
The glories of His righteousness,
The wonders of His love,
The wonders of His love,
The wonders, wonders of His love.

709 Jesus, You are the power

Words and music
Dave Fellingham

C
G/B
Am7
C/G
Je - sus, You are the power, You are the wis - dom That
Fmaj7
Em7
Dm7
G
comes from the Lord God, Who has re-vealed His love.
C
G/B
Am
Fm6/A♭
Our faith now rests on Your power Lord, Which Your
C/G
G
C
Spi - rit has poured out on us.

C
Am7
We___ de - clare__ the mys-tery hid___ be - fore__ the a - ges,
Fmaj7
Gsus
G
Which God had planned___ for our glo - ry.
E7
Am
G
For___ we______ have re - ceived a
G/F
Em7
C/E
Dm7
glo - rious in - he - ri - tance__ Pledged by the

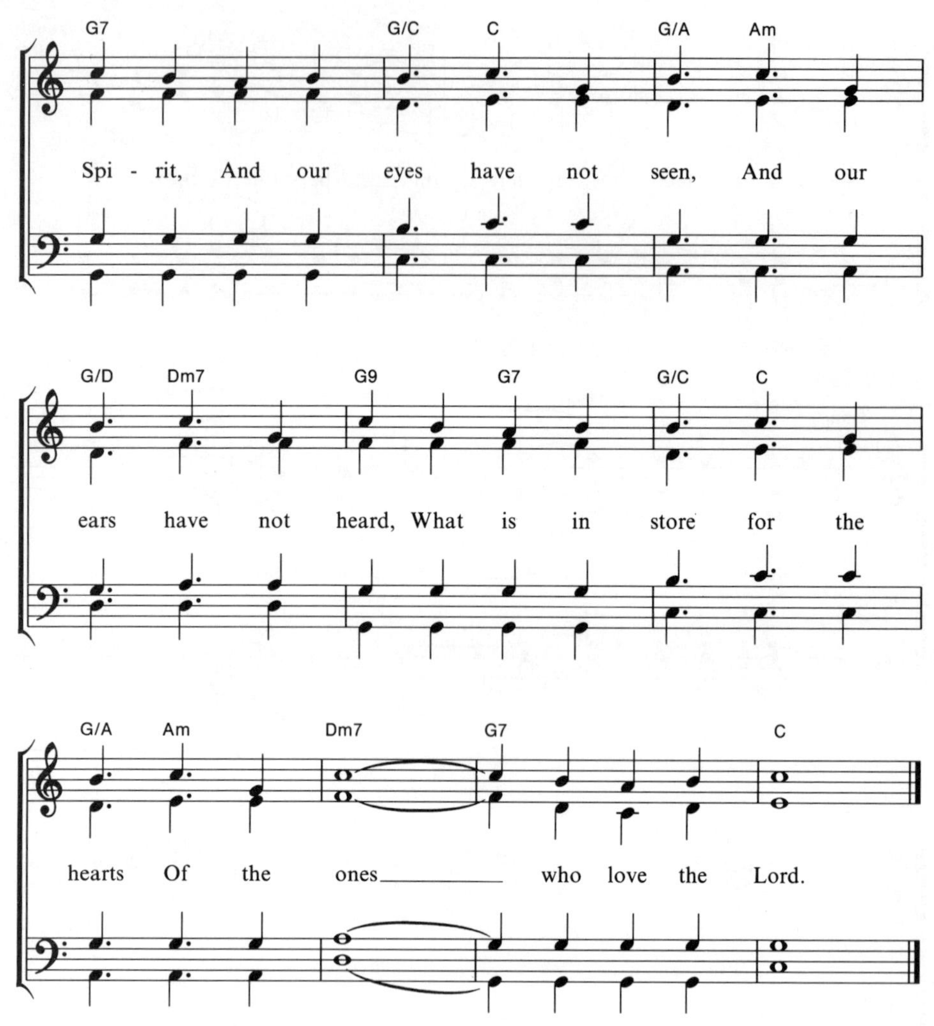
G7
G/C
C
G/A
Am
Spi - rit, And our eyes have not seen, And our
G/D
Dm7
G9
G7
G/C
C
ears have not heard, What is in store for the
G/A
Am
Dm7
G7
C
hearts Of the ones who love the Lord.

Jesus, You are the power,
You are the wisdom
That comes from the Lord God,
Who has revealed His love.

Our faith now rests on Your power Lord,
Which Your Spirit has poured out on us.
We declare the mystery hid before the ages,
Which God had planned for our glory.

For we have received a glorious inheritance
Pledged by the Spirit,
And our eyes have not seen,
And our ears have not heard,
What is in store for the hearts
Of the ones who love the Lord.

710 Jehovah Jireh

Words and music
Merla Watson

Em Am C D

Je-ho-vah Jir - eh, my Pro-vi - der, His grace is suf - fi-cient for__

1. Em B Em B Em 2. Em G

me, for me, for me. me. My God shall sup - ply__ all my

Am D7 G B7

needs____ Ac - cord-ing to His rich - es in glo - ry.

Em Am Cmaj7 D

He will give His an - gels__ charge ov - er me. Je - ho-vah Jir-eh cares for__

Em B7 Em B7 B C D Em

me, for me, for me. Je - ho-vah Jir - eh cares_ for__ me.

711 Let it be to me

Words and music
Graham Kendrick

Gently flowing
G/A
D
Bm7
Em7
A
Let it be to me ac - cord - ing to Your
D
F♯m7
Em
A
Word. Let it be to me ac - cord - ing to Your
Dsus
D
F♯sus
F♯
Bm
Bm/A
Word. I am Your ser-vant, no rights shall I de -
Bm/G♯
Gmaj7
D
A/C♯
Bm
Em7
G/A
- mand. Let it be to me, let it be to

D
D/C
G/B
Fdim
F♯m7
Bm
me,
Let it be to me ac -

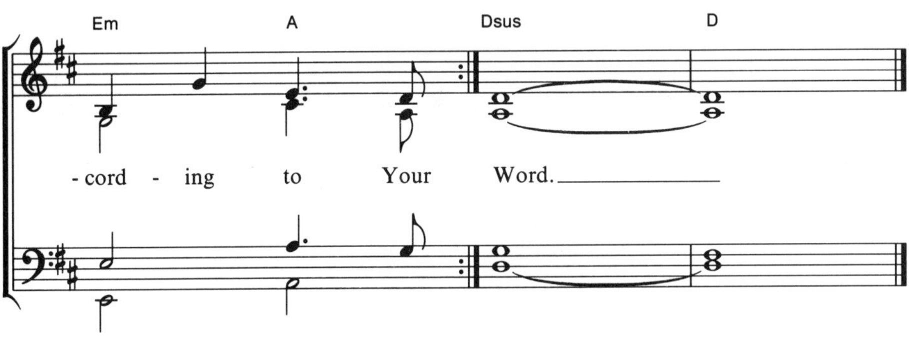
Em
A
Dsus
D
- cord - ing to Your Word.

Let it be to me according to Your Word.
Let it be to me according to Your Word.
I am Your servant, no rights shall I demand.
Let it be to me, let it be to me,
Let it be to me according to Your Word.

712 Like a candle flame

(The candle song)

Words and music
Graham Kendrick

Softly, with awe

Am Em Am Em F G C

C Em7 F G C Am Dm G E7 F G

Like a can - dle flame, Flick-'ring small in our dark-ness.

C Em7 F G C Am Dm G C

Un - cre - a - ted light Shines through in - fant eyes.

𝄋

Am Em F Am Em F

WOMEN: *God is with us, al - le -*

MEN: *God is with us, al - le - lu - ia,*

Am Em F Am Em F G
-lu - ia, Come to save us, Al - le - lu -
Come to save us, al - le - lu - ia, Al - le - lu -

1.2. to next verse
3. D.𝄋
4.
C Dm7 G C C
-ia! -ia! -ia!

1 Like a candle flame,
Flick'ring small in our darkness.
Uncreated light
Shines through infant eyes.
MEN *God is with us, alleluia,*
WOMEN *God is with us, alleluia,*
MEN *Come to save us, alleluia,*
WOMEN *Come to save us,*
ALL *Alleluia!*

2 Stars and angels sing,
Yet the earth
Sleeps in the shadows;
Can this tiny spark
Set a world on fire?
God is with us . . .

3 Yet His light shall shine
From our lives,
Spirit blazing,
As we touch the flame
Of His holy fire.
God is with us . . .

713 Lord we long for You

(Heal our nation)

Words and music
Trish Morgan, Ray Goudie,
Ian Townend, Dave Bankhead

Prayerfully, with feeling
Capo 2(D)
E (D) A (G) E/B (D/A) B (A)
Lord we long for You to move in pow - er.
F♯m7 (Em7) B7 (A7) A/B (G/A) E (D) B/D♯ (A/C♯)
There's a hun - ger deep with - in our hearts,
C♯m (Bm) G♯m7 (F♯m7) F♯m7 (Em7) E/G♯ (D/F♯)
To see heal-ing in our na-tion. Send Your Spi-rit to re -
Asus2 (Gsus2) B9 (A9) E (D) Esus2/G♯ (Dsus2/F♯) Asus2 (Gsus2) A/B (G/A)
- vive us: Heal our na - tion!

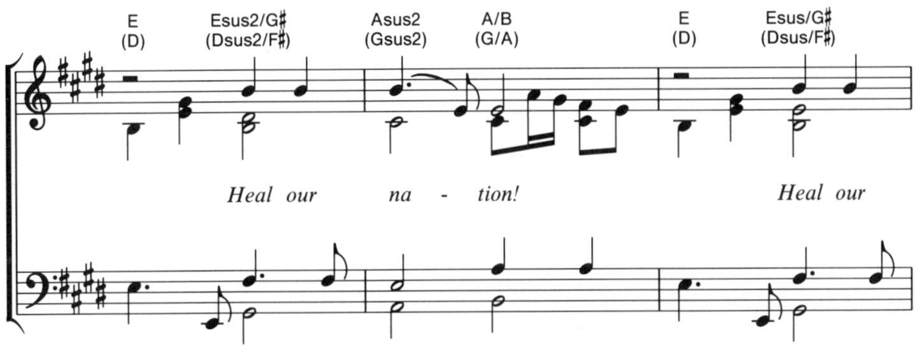
E
(D)
Esus2/G♯
(Dsus2/F♯)
Asus2
(Gsus2)
A/B
(G/A)
E
(D)
Esus/G♯
(Dsus/F♯)
Heal our na - tion! Heal our

Asus2
(Gsus2)
A/B
(G/A)
F♯m7
(Em7)
B9
(A9)
E
(D)
na - tion! Pour out Your Spi - rit on this land!

1 Lord we long for You to move in power.
There's a hunger deep within our hearts,
To see healing in our nation.
Send Your Spirit to revive us:
Heal our nation!
Heal our nation!
Heal our nation!
Pour out Your Spirit on this land!

2 Lord we hear Your Spirit coming closer,
A mighty wave to break upon our land,
Bringing justice, and forgiveness,
God we cry to You 'Revive us':
Heal our nation . . .

714 Lord, the light of Your love

Words and music
Graham Kendrick

Majestic and steady
Capo 2(G)
A (G) D/A (C/G) E/A (D/G) D/A (C/G) A (G) D/A (C/G) E/A (D/G) D/A (C/G)
A (G) Asus (Gsus) A (G) E/A (D/G) A (G) Asus (Gsus)
Lord, the light of Your love is shin - ing, In the midst of the
A (G) E/A (D/G) D (C) E/D (D) C♯m (Bm) F♯m (Em)
dark - ness, shin - ing: Je - sus, light of the world, shine up - on us;
D (C) E/D (D) C♯m (Bm) F♯m (Em) G (F) Esus (Dsus) E (D)
Set us free by the truth You now bring us – shine on me,

A (G) E/A (D/G) A (G) D (C) A (G) Bm (Am) Bm/A (Am7/G)
Shine, Jesus, shine, Fill this land with the
Flow, river, flow, Flood the nations with
Esus (Dsus) E (D) A (G) E/A (D/G) A (G) D (C) A (G)
1. Bm (Am) Bm/A (Am7/G)
Father's glory; Blaze, Spirit, blaze, Set our hearts on
grace and mercy; Send forth Your word, Lord, And
G (F) Esus (Dsus) E (D)
2. Bm (Am) E7 (D7) A (G) D/A (C)
D.𝄋
last time
A (G)
fire.
let there be light!

1 Lord, the light of Your love is shining,
In the midst of the darkness, shining:
Jesus, light of the world, shine upon us;
Set us free by the truth You now bring us –
Shine on me, shine on me.
Shine, Jesus, shine,
Fill this land with the Father's glory;
Blaze, Spirit, blaze,
Set our hearts on fire.
Flow, river, flow,
Flood the nations with grace and mercy;
Send forth Your word, Lord,
And let there be light!

2 Lord, I come to Your awesome presence,
From the shadows into Your radiance;
By Your Blood I may enter Your brightness:
Search me, try me, consume all my darkness –
Shine on me, shine on me.
Shine, Jesus, shine . . .

3 As we gaze on Your kingly brightness
So our faces display Your likeness,
Ever changing from glory to glory:
Mirrored here, may our lives tell Your story –
Shine on me, shine on me.
Shine, Jesus, shine . . .

715 Lord, I love You

Words and music
Eddie Espinosa

With feeling
G C/G G
Lord, I love You, You a-lone did
Am/F♯ B7 Em7
hear my cry, On - ly You can mend this
Dm7 G7 C G/C C
bro - ken heart of mine. Yes, I
Cm6 C/G G
love You, And there is no doubt,

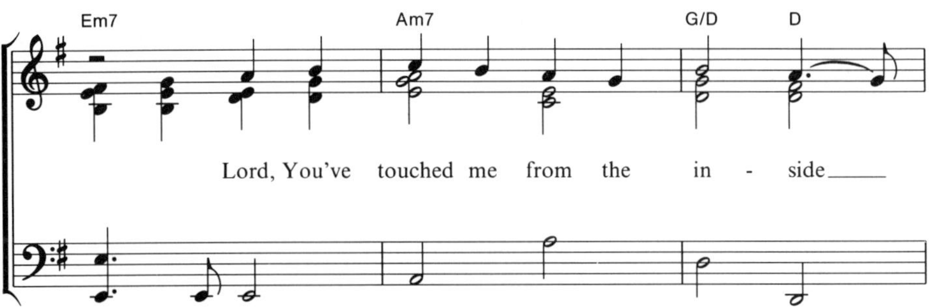
Em7
Am7
G/D
D
Lord, You've touched me from the in - side

1.
G
D
2.
G
C/D
G
out.
Lord, I
out.

Lord, I love You
You alone did hear my cry,
Only You can mend this broken heart of mine.
Yes, I love You,
And there is no doubt,
Lord, You've touched me from the inside out.

716 Lord, come and heal Your church

Words and music
Chris Rolinson

Worshipfully
D A/C♯ Bm F♯m/A
1 Lord, come and heal Your church, Take our lives and
2 Spi - rit of God, come in And re - lease our
3 Show us Your power, we pray, That__ we may
G Em D/A Asus A D A/C♯
cleanse with Your fi - re; Let Your de-liver - ance
hearts to__ praise You; Make us__ whole, for
share in Your glo - ry: We shall a - rise, and
Bm F♯m/A G Em D/A Asus A/G
flow As we lift Your name up__ high - er.
Ho - ly__ we'll be - come and__ serve You,
go To pro-claim Your works most_ ho - ly.
F♯sus F♯ Bm Bm/A G D/F♯
We will draw near And sur - ren - der our__

Em7
A
A/G
D/F♯
Fdim
fear: Lift our hands to pro - claim, 'Ho - ly
Em7
D/F♯
G
G/A
A
D
Fa - ther, You are___ here!'

1 Lord, come and heal Your church,
Take our lives and cleanse with Your fire;
Let Your deliverance flow
As we lift Your name up higher.
We will draw near
And surrender our fear:
Lift our hands to proclaim,
'Holy Father, You are here!'

2 Spirit of God, come in
And release our hearts to praise You;
Make us whole, for
Holy we'll become and serve You,
We will draw near . . .

3 Show us Your power, we pray,
That we may share in Your glory:
We shall arise, and go
To proclaim Your works most holy.
We will draw near . . .

717 Look to the skies

Words and music
Graham Kendrick

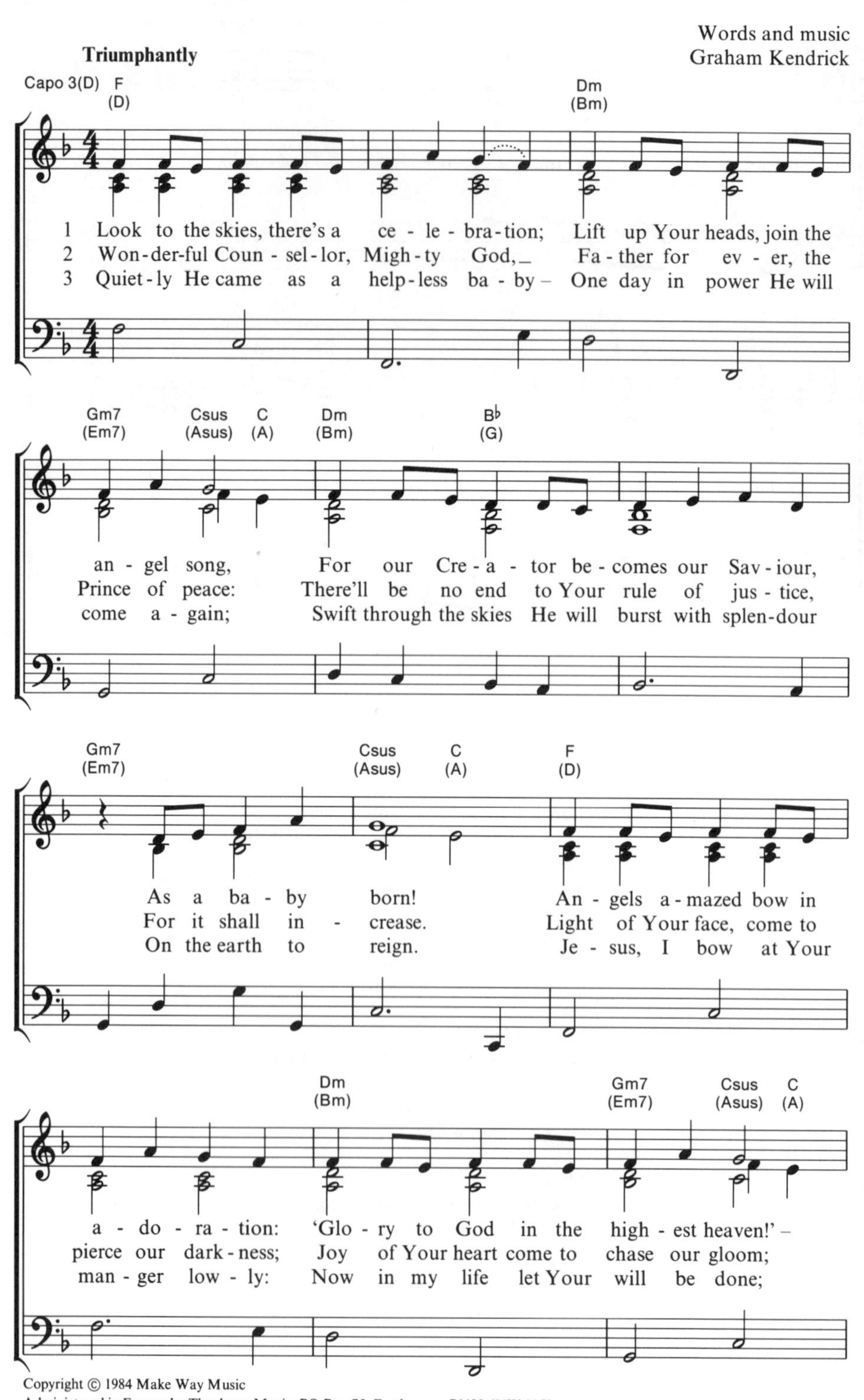
Triumphantly
Capo 3(D)
F (D)
Dm (Bm)
1 Look to the skies, there's a ce - le - bra - tion; Lift up Your heads, join the
2 Won - der - ful Coun - sel - lor, Migh - ty God, Fa - ther for ev - er, the
3 Quiet - ly He came as a help - less ba - by – One day in power He will
Gm7 (Em7)
Csus (Asus)
C (A)
Bb (G)
an - gel song, For our Cre - a - tor be - comes our Sav - iour,
Prince of peace: There'll be no end to Your rule of jus - tice,
come a - gain; Swift through the skies He will burst with splen - dour
As a ba - by born! An - gels a - mazed bow in
For it shall in - crease. Light of Your face, come to
On the earth to reign. Je - sus, I bow at Your
a - do - ra - tion: 'Glo - ry to God in the high - est heaven!' –
pierce our dark - ness; Joy of Your heart come to chase our gloom;
man - ger low - ly: Now in my life let Your will be done;

Dm (Bm) B♭ (G) Gm (Em) Csus (Asus) C (A)
Send the good news out to ev - ery na - tion, For our hope has come.
Star of the morn-ing, a new day dawn-ing, Make our hearts Your home.
Live in my flesh by Your Spi - rit ho - ly Till Your King - dom comes.
Dm (Bm) Gm (Em) C (A) Dm (Bm)
Wor - ship the King – come, see His bright-ness; Wor - ship the King, His
B♭ (G) Csus (Asus) C (A) Dm (Bm) B♭ (G) C (A)
won - ders tell: Je - sus our King is born to - day – We
Gm7 (Em7) C9 (A9) C (A) F (D)
wel-come You, Em - man - u - el!

718 Let all the earth

Words and music
Graham Kendrick

Lively
C G/B Am Am/G D/F♯
Gsus G C G/B Am Am/G
Let all the earth hear His voice, Let the peo-ple re-
D/F♯ Gsus G C G/B
-joice At the sound of His name; Let all the val-leys and
Am Am/G D/F♯ Gsus G
hills burst with joy, And the trees of the field Clap their hands.

F
G
E7
Am
F
G
Just-ice and love He will bring to the world, His king-dom will nev - er
C
(E)
F
G
E7
Am
fail; Held like a two-ed-ged sword in our hand,
Fmaj7
Gsus
G
His word and truth shall pre - vail, shall pre -
To end
C
F
C
G
C
- vail!

1 Let all the earth hear His voice,
Let the people rejoice
At the sound of His name;
Let all the valleys and hills burst with joy,
And the trees of the field
Clap their hands.
Justice and love He will bring to the world,
His kingdom will never fail;
Held like a two-edged sword in our hand,
His word and truth shall prevail, shall prevail!

2 Let all the earth hear His voice,
Let the prisoners rejoice –
He is coming to save.
Satan's dark strongholds crash down
As with prayer we surround,
As the cross we proclaim.
Justice and love . . .

3 Let all the earth hear His song;
Sing it loud, sing it strong –
It's the song of His praise.
Silent no more, we cry out –
Let the world hear the shout:
In the earth the Lord reigns.
Justice and love . . .

719 Light has dawned

Strongly
Words and music
Graham Kendrick
Capo 2(G)
F♯m (Em) E (D) Bm (Am) F♯m (Em) E (D) F♯sus (Esus) F♯ (E) Bm (Am) Esus (Dsus) E (D)
A (G) E/A (D/G) A (G) A (G) E/A (D/G) D/A (C) F♯m (Em)
1 Light has dawned that ev - er shall blaze,
WOMEN 2 Sav - iour of the world is___ He,
MEN 3 Life has sprung from hearts of___ stone,
4 Blood has flowed that cleans - es from sin,
Dmaj7 (Cmaj7) D/E (C) Esus (Dsus) E (D) A (G) E/A (D)
Dark - ness flees a - way; Christ the light has
Hea - ven's King come down; Judge-ment, love and
By the Spi - rit's breath; Hell shall let her
God His love has proved; Man may mock and
D/A (C) F♯m (Em) Dmaj7 (Cmaj7) Esus (Dsus) E7 (D7) A (G) Asus (Gsus) A (G)
shone in our hearts, Turn - ing night to day.
mer - cy___ meet At His thor - ny crown.
cap - tives_ go, Life has con-quered death.
dem - ons may rage - We shall not be moved!

F♯m (Em) E (D) Bm (Am) F♯m (Em) E (D) A (G) F♯m (Em) E (D) Bm (Am)
ALL
We pro - claim Him King of kings, We lift high His
Esus (Dsus) E (D) F♯m (Em) E (D) Bm (Am) F♯m (Em) E (D) F♯sus (Esus) F♯ (E)
name; Heaven and earth shall bow at His feet,
Bm (Am) Esus (Dsus) E (D)
1-3.
Asus (Gsus) A (G) E/A (D/G) A (G)
When He comes to reign.
4.
Asus (Gsus) A (G)
D.S.
5.
A (G) D/A (C/G) E/A (D/G) D/A (C/G) A (G)
reign. reign.

720 May our worship be acceptable

Words and music
Graham Kendrick

Prayerfully
Capo 2(D)
E (D) Emaj7 (Dmaj7) E6 (D6) Emaj7 (Dmaj7) Amaj7 (Gmaj7) A/B (G/A)
May our wor - ship be ac-cept-a-ble_ In Your sight, O
E (D) A/B (G/A) B (A) E (D) Emaj7 (Dmaj7) E6 (D6) Emaj7 (Dmaj7)
Lord; May our wor - ship be ac-cept-a-ble_
Amaj7 (Gmaj7) A/B (G/A) B6 (A6) E (D) D/E (C/D) E7 (D7) Amaj7 (Gmaj7) B/A (A/G)
In Your sight, O Lord; May the words of my
G♯m7 (F♯m7) C♯m7 (Bm7) F♯9 (E9) Amaj7 (Gmaj7)
mouth be pure, And the me - di - ta - tion

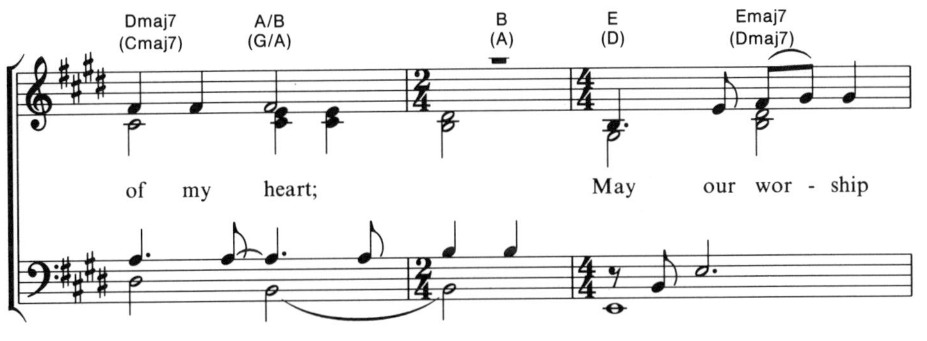
Dmaj7
(Cmaj7)
A/B
(G/A)
B
(A)
E
(D)
Emaj7
(Dmaj7)
of my heart; May our wor - ship

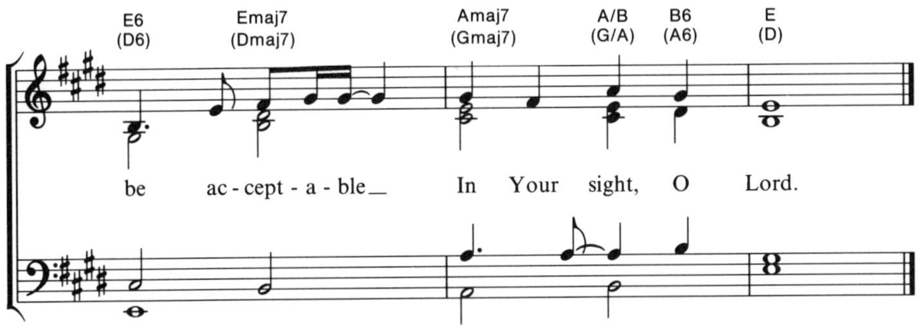
E6
(D6)
Emaj7
(Dmaj7)
Amaj7
(Gmaj7)
A/B
(G/A)
B6
(A6)
E
(D)
be ac - cept - a - ble_ In Your sight, O Lord.

May our worship be acceptable
  In Your sight, O Lord;
May our worship be acceptable
  In Your sight, O Lord;
May the words of my mouth be pure,
  And the meditation of my heart;
May our worship be acceptable
  In Your sight, O Lord.

721 Mighty in victory

Words and music
Mavis Ford

Hebrew style
Capo 5(C) Dm (Am)
Gm (Dm)
Migh - ty in vic - tory, glo - rious in ma - je - sty:
A (E)
Dm (Am) Dm/C (Am/G) B♭ (F) A7 (E7)
Ev - ery eye shall see Him when He ap - pears,
Dm (Am)
Gm (Dm)
Com - ing in the clouds with pow - er and glo - ry.
A (E)
Dm (Am)
D (A)
Hail to the King! We must be rea - dy,

Gm (Dm) Gm/F (Dm/C) Gm/E (Dm/B) G7/D (D7/A) C (G)
watch - ing and pray - ing, Serv - ing each o - ther, —
F (C) Gm (Dm) Dm/A (Am) A (E) Dm (Am)
build - ing His king - dom; Then ev - ery knee shall bow,
Gm (Dm) A (E) Dm (Am)
then ev - ery tongue con - fess, Je - sus is Lord!

Mighty in victory, glorious in majesty:
Every eye shall see Him when He appears,
Coming in the clouds with power and glory.
  Hail to the King!
We must be ready, watching and praying,
Serving each other, building His kingdom;
Then every knee shall bow, then every tongue confess,
  Jesus is Lord!

722 Now dawns the Sun of righteousness

(Tell out the news)

Words and music
Graham Kendrick

Joyful and bright
Am G F C C/B Am Em
1 Now dawns the Sun of_ right-eous-ness, And the dark-ness will ne - ver His
2 Laugh - ter and joy He will in-crease, All our bur-dens be lift - ed, Op -
3 So let us go, His wit - ness - es, Spread-ing news of His king-dom Of
F C/E B♭ G Am G F C C/B
bright-ness dim; True light that lights the hearts of men, On - ly
- press - ion cease; The blood-stained bat - tle - dress be burned, And the
right-eous-ness, 'Till the whole world has heard the song, 'Till the
Am Em F C/E Dm C B♭ Gsus G
Son of the Fa - ther, Je - sus Christ.
art of our war - fare Ne - ver more be learned.
har - vest is ga-thered, Then the end shall come.
Tell
C G C F C/E Dm C G
out, tell out_ the_ news, On ev - ery street pro-claim, A___

Am
C
G
Am
D
D7
G
child is born, a Son is given And Je - sus is His Name! Tell
C
G
C
F
C/E
Dm
C
G
out, tell out_ the_ news, Our Sav - iour Christ has come, In_
Am
C
G
Am
D
E7
Am
ev - ery tribe and na - tion, Let songs of praise be sung, Let
Dm7
Gsus
G
C
D.C.
songs of praise be sung!
3rd time only
or end

723 O come and join the dance

Words and music
Graham Kendrick
As a Scottish folk-dance
D(no 3rd) C/D A/D D(no 3rd)C/D D(no 3rd) D(no 3rd)
1. 2.
LEADER
1 O
D Am7 A7
come and join the dance That all be - gan so long a - go,___ When
(2) shed your hea - vy load And dance your wor - ries all a - way,___ For
(3) Instrumental
(4) laugh - ter ring and an - gels sing And joy be all a - round,_ For
ALL
D Am7 D
Christ the Lord was born in Beth - le - hem. Through
Christ the Lord was born in Beth - le - hem. He
Christ the Lord was born in Beth - le - hem. And
LEADER
D Am7 A7
all the years of dark - ness Still the dance goes on and on,___ Oh,
came to break the power of sin And turn your night to day,___ Oh,
if you seek with all your heart He sure - ly can be found,_ Oh,
ALL

D
Am7
D
take my hand and come and join the song.
MEN: Re -
take my hand and come and join the song.
take my hand and come and join the song.
Am7
A7
- joice! Re-joice! O lift your voice and sing, And
WOMEN: Re - joice! Re - joice!
D
Am7
D
o-pen up your heart to wel-come Him.
MEN: Re-joice! Re-joice! And
WOMEN: Re-joice! Re-joice!
1.2.3.
Am7
A7
D
Am7
D
wel-come now your King, For Christ the Lord was born in Beth-le - hem.
LEADER
2 Come
3
4 Let

D.𝄋
4. D
5. D
D
Am7
- hem.
MEN: Re -
- hem.
For Christ the Lord was born in Beth-le -
D
Am7
D C/D D
- hem.
For Christ the Lord was born in Beth - le - hem.

1 LEADER O come and join the dance
That all began so long ago,
ALL When Christ the Lord was born in Bethlehem.
LEADER Through all the years of darkness
Still the dance goes on and on,
ALL Oh, take my hand and come and join the song.
MEN *Rejoice!*
WOMEN *Rejoice!*
MEN *Rejoice!*
WOMEN *Rejoice!*
ALL *O lift your voice and sing,*
And open up your heart to welcome Him.
MEN *Rejoice!*
WOMEN *Rejoice!*
MEN *Rejoice!*
WOMEN *Rejoice!*
ALL *And welcome now your King,*
For Christ the Lord was born in Bethlehem.

2 LEADER Come shed your heavy load
And dance your worries all away,
ALL For Christ the Lord was born in Bethlehem.
LEADER He came to break the power of sin
And turn your night to day,
ALL Oh, take my hand and come and join the song.
Rejoice . . .

3 *(Instrumental verse and chorus)*

4 LEADER Let laughter ring and angels sing
And joy be all around,
ALL For Christ the Lord was born in Bethlehem.
LEADER And if you seek with all your heart
He surely can be found,
ALL Oh, take my hand and come and join the song.
Rejoice . . .
Rejoice . . .
For Christ the Lord was born in Bethlehem.
For Christ the Lord was born in Bethlehem.

724 Oh, the joy of Your forgiveness

Words and Music
Dave Bilbrough

Slow 4
Capo 3(G)
B♭ (G) Dm (Bm) Cm7 (Am) F (D)
Oh, the joy of Your for - give - ness,
B♭ (G) Dm (Bm) Cm7 (Am) D7 (B7) Gm (Em) Gm/F (Em/D)
Slow - ly sweep-ing o - ver me; Now in heart-felt a - do -
Gm7 (Am) F (D) Cm7 (Am) F (D) B♭/D (G/B)
- ra - tion This praise I'll bring
Cm7 (Am) F (D) B♭/D (G/B) Cm7 (Am) F7 (D) B♭sus4 (G) B♭ (G)
to You my King, I'll wor-ship You my Lord.

725 Oh what a mystery I see

Words and music
Graham Kendrick
Brightly, quite quick
D A/C♯ Bm D/A Em/B Em D/A A7 D
f
1 O
D Bm A Bm A G Asus A
what a mys - te - ry I see, What mar - vel - lous de -
(2) per - fect Man, in - car - nate God, By self - less sac - ri -
WOMEN (3) faith a child of His I stand, An heir in Da - vid's
D Bm A Bm A
- sign, That God should come as one of us, A
- fice De - stroyed our sin - ful hi - sto - ry, All
line, Roy - al de - scend - ant by His blood Des -
G Asus A D G D
Son in Da - vid's line. Flesh of our flesh, of
fall - en Ad - am's curse. In Him the curse to
- tined by Love's de - sign. MEN: Fa - thers of faith, my

G D G D/F♯ Em7 Bm Asus
wo - man born, Our hu - man - ness He owns;
bless - ing turns, My bar - ren spi - rit flowers,
fa - thers now! Be - cause in Christ I am,
A D Bm A Bm A
And for a world of wick - ed - ness His
As ov - er the shatter - ed power of sin The
ALL: And all God's pro - mis - es in Him To
G Asus A
1.2.
D A/C♯ Bm D/A
guilt - less blood a - tones.
cross of Je - sus towers.
me are 'Yes, A - men!'
Em/B Em D/A A7 D
3.
D B♭7
2 This
WOMEN 3 By
men! 4 No

Capo 1(D)
E♭ (D) Cm (Bm) B♭ (A) Cm (Bm) B♭ (A) A♭ (G) B♭sus (Asus) B♭ (A)
more then_ as a child of earth Must I my life - time
E♭ (D) Cm (Bm) B♭ (A) Cm (Bm) B♭ (A)
spend – His his - to - ry, His des - ti - ny Are
A♭ (G) B♭sus (Asus) B♭ (A) E♭ (D) A♭ (G) E♭ (D)
mine to ap - pre - hend. Oh what_ a___ Sav - iour,
A♭ (G) E♭ (D) A♭ (G) E♭/G (D/F♯) Fm7 (Em7) Cm (Bm) B♭sus (Asus)
what_ a___ Lord, O Mast - er, Bro - ther, Friend!___

B♭
(A)
E♭
(D)
Cm
(Bm)
B♭
(A)
Cm
(Bm)
B♭
(A)
— What mi - ra - cle has joined me to This
A♭
(G)
B♭sus
(Asus)
B♭
(A)
E♭
(D)
life that ne - ver ends!
A♭
(G)
B♭
(A)
E♭
(D)

1 O what a mystery I see,
What marvellous design,
That God should come as one of us,
A Son in David's line.
Flesh of our flesh, of woman born,
Our humanness He owns;
And for a world of wickedness
His guiltless blood atones.

2 This perfect Man, incarnate God,
By selfless sacrifice
Destroyed our sinful history,
All fallen Adam's curse.
In Him the curse to blessing turns,
My barren spirit flowers,
As over the shattered power of sin
The cross of Jesus towers.

WOMEN
3 By faith a child of His I stand,
An heir in David's line,
Royal descendant by His blood
Destined by Love's design.
MEN
Fathers of faith, my fathers now!
Because in Christ I am,
ALL
And all God's promises in Him
To me are 'Yes, Amen'!

4 No more then as a child of earth
Must I my lifetime spend –
His history, His destiny
Are mine to apprehend.
Oh what a Saviour, what a Lord,
O Master, Brother, Friend!
What miracle has joined me to
This life that never ends!

726 Oh Lord

Words: Greg Leavers
Music: Greg Leavers and Phil Burt

D9
D
D9
D
Oh Lord, I turn my mind to You Right a -
Oh Lord, I turn my eyes to You And see
Oh Lord, please speak Your Word to me, Just the
Oh Lord, please fill my heart a - new; I sur -

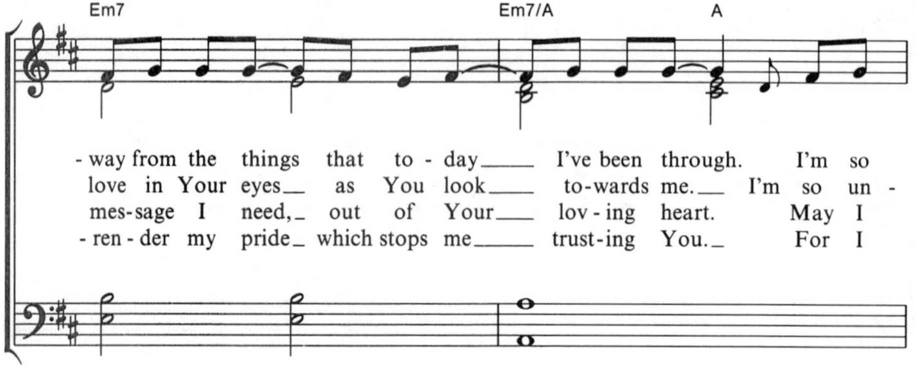
Em7
Em7/A
A
- way from the things that to - day I've been through. I'm so
love in Your eyes as You look to-wards me. I'm so un -
mes-sage I need, out of Your lov - ing heart. May I
- ren - der my pride which stops me trust-ing You. For I

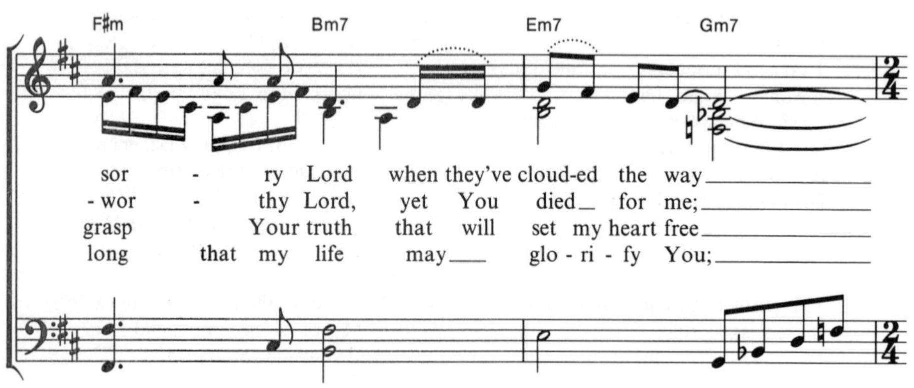
F♯m
Bm7
Em7
Gm7
sor - ry Lord when they've cloud-ed the way
- wor - thy Lord, yet You died for me;
grasp Your truth that will set my heart free
long that my life may glo - ri - fy You;

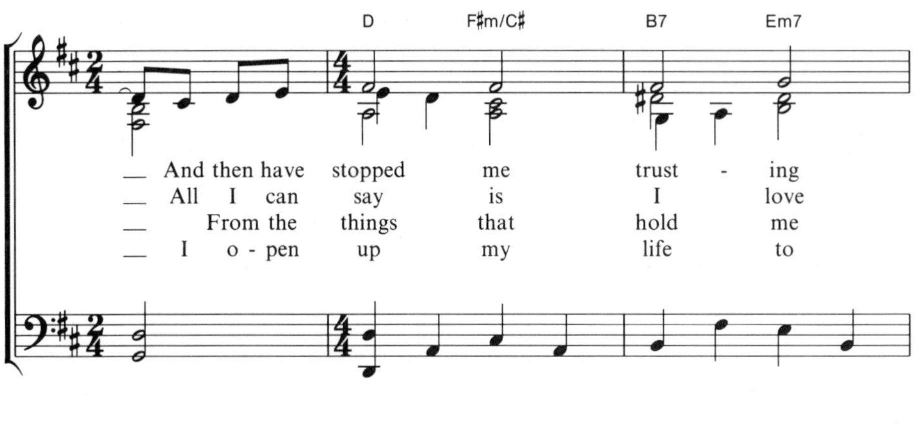
D
F#m/C#
B7
Em7
__ And then have stopped me trust - ing
__ All I can say is I love
__ From the things that hold me
__ I o - pen up my life to

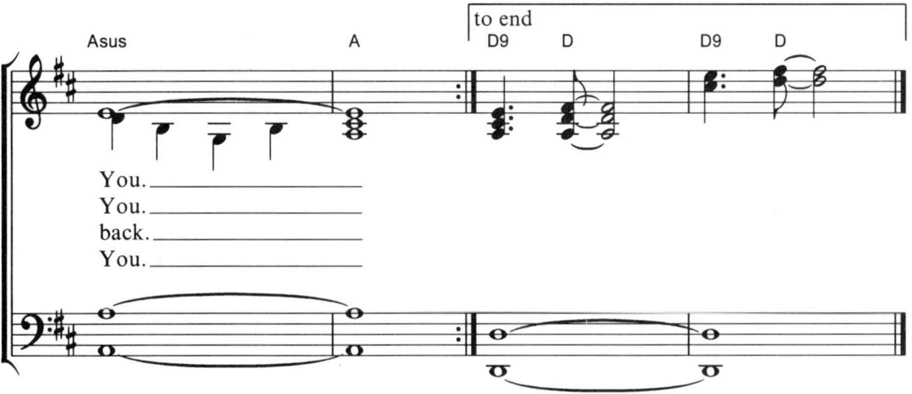
to end
Asus
A
D9
D
D9
D
You. ___
You. ___
back. ___
You. ___

1 Oh Lord, I turn my mind to You
Right away from the things that today I've been through.
I'm so sorry Lord when they've clouded the way
And then have stopped me trusting You.

2 Oh Lord, I turn my eyes to You
And see love in Your eyes as You look towards me.
I'm so unworthy Lord, yet You died for me;
All I can say is I love You.

3 Oh Lord, please speak Your Word to me,
Just the message I need, out of Your loving heart.
May I grasp Your truth that will set my heart free
From the things that hold me back.

4 Oh Lord, please fill my heart anew;
I surrender my pride which stops me trusting You.
For I long that my life may glorify You;
I open up my life to You.

727 O Lord, our Lord

(How majestic is Your name)

Words and music
Michael Smith

Joyously

mf

D | G Em7 D/F♯ | D | A A9/C♯ D | | G Em7 D/F♯

D | A A9/C♯ D |

O Lord, our Lord, How ma -

G Em7 D/F♯ | D | A A9/C♯ D

- jes - tic is Your name in all___ the___ earth; O

D | G Em7 D/F♯ | D

Lord, our Lord, How maj - es - tic is Your name in all___ the___

A A9/C♯ D
G
Em7
A G/B A7/C♯
earth; O Lord, we praise Your
D
G
Em7
A G/B A7/C♯
name; O Lord, we mag-ni-fy Your
D C♯ F♯m E A A/G D/F♯ G
name. Prince of peace, migh-ty God, O Lord God al-
to repeat
Asus A D G D/F♯
-migh - ty!
last time
Asus A D G Em7 D/F♯ D
migh - ty!

728 O Lord, the clouds are gathering

Words and music
Graham Kendrick

With strength
C G/B Am Em7
1 O___ Lord,___ the clouds are gath - er - ing, The fire of judge-ment
(2) Lord,___ ov - er the na - tions now, Where is the dove of
(3) Lord,___ dark powers are poised to flood Our streets with hate and
(4) Lord,___ Your glo - rious cross shall tower Tri - um - phant in this
Fmaj7 C/G G C G/B
burns.___ How we have fal - len! O___ Lord,___ You stand ap -
peace?___ Her wings are bro - ken, O___ Lord,___ while pre-cious
fear.___ We must a - wak - en! O___ Lord,___ let love re -
land,___ E - vil con - found - ing; Through the fire,___ Your suf-fering
Am Em7 Fmaj7 Dm7 C/G G
- palled to see Your laws of love so scorned. And lives so bro - ken.
chil - dren starve, The tools of war in - crease,_ Their bread is sto - len.
- claim the lives That sin would sweep a - way,___ And let Your king-dom come!
church dis - play The glo - ries of her Christ,_ Prais - es re - sound - ing.
Am Am/G F C/E
WOMEN Have mer-cy, Lord,___ For-give us, Lord. Re -
MEN Have mer-cy, Lord,___ For - give us, Lord,___ Re -

B/F♯ B7/D♯ Esus E
-store us, Lord; Re-vive Your church a - gain.
-store us, Lord; Re-vive Your church a - gain. Let
Am Am/G F C/E
Let jus-tice flow, Like ri - vers; And
jus-tice flow, Like ri - vers, And
Gsus/D D7 Gsus G
ALL
right-eous-ness Like a ne - ver - fail - ing stream.
1.2.3.
4.
F/G G F/G G C G/C F/C C
2 O
3 O
4 Yet, O
A ne-ver fail-ing stream.

729 Open your eyes

Words and music
Carl Tuttle

Worshipfully
C G/C F G C F/C
O - pen your_ eyes, See the glo - ry of the King;
C G/C F G C
Lift up your_ voice, And His prais - es_____ sing!
F G C F G C
I love You, Lord, I will pro-claim:
F G Am7 F Dm7 G C
Al - le - lu - ia! I bless Your name.

730 Peace to you

Words and music
Graham Kendrick

A Asus A D/A A
Peace to you. We bless you now __ in the name of the
E/A A Asus A D/A A
Lord. Peace to you. We bless you now __ in the name of the
repeat verse 3 times
E/A F♯m E A Asus A
Prince of Peace. Peace to you. Peace to
rit.
A Asus A E/A A Asus A E/A A
you. Peace to you. Peace to you. ______

731 Rejoice, rejoice, rejoice

Words and music
Chris Bowater

Lively
D
Dsus
D
Dsus
Re - joice,
re - joice,
re - joice,
Re - joice,
D
Dsus
D
Dsus
D
re - joice,
re - joice;
My soul
re - joi -
last time to Coda
A7
D
Dsus
D
Dsus
- ces in
the Lord.
D7
Gmaj7
A7
My
soul
mag - ni - fies
the Lord,

F♯m7
Bm7
Em7
And my spi - rit re -
A7
D
Em
Ddim/F
D/F♯
D7
-joi - ces in God my Sav - iour; My
Gmaj7
A7
F♯m7
soul mag - ni - fies the Lord,
Bm7
E7
And my spi - rit re - joi - ces in my
D.C. al Coda
CODA
Asus
A
A7
D
Dsus
D
God.

732 Reigning in all splendour

Words and music
Dave Bilborough

Majestically
Capo 5(Am)
Dm (Am) C (G) B♭ (F) F (C) Dm (Am) C (G)
Reign-ing in all splen - dour – Vic - tor - i - ous love;
Gm (Dm) C (G) Dm (Am) C (G) B♭ (F) F (C)
— Christ Je - sus the Sav - iour,
Dm (Am) C (G) Gm (Dm) C (G) B♭ (F) C (G)
Tran-scen-dent a - bove. — All earth-ly dom-in -
Dm (Am) C (G) B♭ (F) C (G) Dm (Am) C (G)
- ions And king-doms shall fall, —

B♭
(F)
Dm
(Am)
C
(G)
B♭
(F)
C
(G)
For His name is Je - sus
And He is the Lord.
A
(E)
Dm
(Am)
Am7/C
(Em7/G)
He is Lord,
B♭
(F)
C
(G)
Dm
(Am)
Am7/C
(Em7/G)
B♭
(F)
C
(G)
He is Lord,
He is
Dm
(Am)
Am7/C
(Em7/G)
1.
B♭
(F)
C
(G)
Dm
(Am)
Am7/C
(Em7/G)
Lord,
He is Lord.
B♭
(F)
C
(G)
2.
B♭
(F)
C
(G)
Dm
(Am)
He is Lord.

733 Swing wide the gates

Words and music
Chris Bowater

G
D/F♯
Em7
Swing wide the gates,

Am7
D
G
Let the King come in.

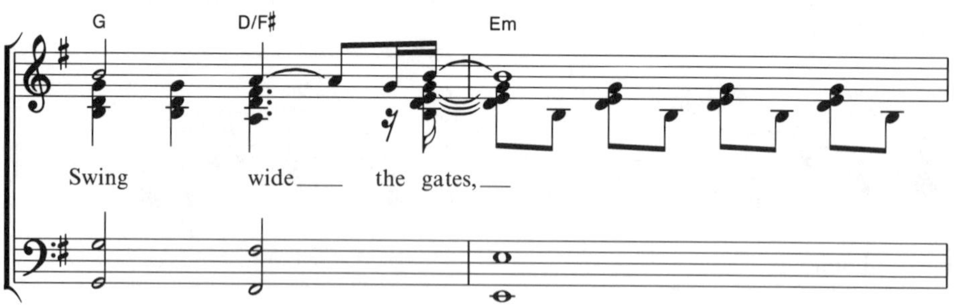
G
D/F♯
Em
Swing wide the gates,

1.
2.
Am
D
G
C/D
G
C/D
Make a way for Him.
Here He comes,

G
Dm/F
Em7
The King of glo - ry; Here He comes,
Am7
Cm/A
3
Migh - ty in vic - to - ry; Here He comes
G
Em
3
C
In splend-our and ma - jes - ty.
G
D
C
C/D
G
Swing wide the gates, Swing wide the gates. Let the King come in,
G
D
C
C/D
G
Swing wide the gates, Swing wide the gates, Let the King come in.

734 Show Your power, O Lord

Words and music
Graham Kendrick

With energy
Capo 2(G)
A (G) D (C) A/E (G) E7 (D7) A (G) Asus (Gsus) A (G) D/A (C)
A (G) D (C)
1 Show Your power, O Lord, De - mon - strate the just -
2 Show Your power, O Lord, Cause Your church to rise
A/E (G/D) E7 (D7) A (G) C♯m7 (Bm7)
- ice of Your king-dom; Prove Your migh - ty word,
and take ac - tion; Let all fear be gone,
A (G) D (C) A/E (G/D) E7 (D7) A (G) Asus (Gsus) A (G)
Vin-di - cate Your name Be-fore a watch-ing world.
Pow-ers of the age To come are break-ing through.

D (C) E/D (D) C♯m7 (Bm7) F♯m7 (Em7)
Awe - some are Your deeds, O Lord – Re -
We Your peo - ple are rea - dy to serve, To a -
B7 (A7) D/E (C/D) E (D)
- new them for this hour.
- rise and to o - bey.
1.
A (G) D (C) A/E (G/D) E7 (D7) A (G) Asus (Gsus) A (G)
Show Your power, O Lord – a-mong the peo-ple now.
2.
A (G) D (C) A/E (G/D) E7 (D7) A (G) D (C)
Show Your power, O Lord, And set the peo-ple; Show Your power, O Lord,
A/E (G/D) E7 (D7) A (G) Asus (Gsus) A (G)
And set the peo - ple free.

735 Such love

Words and music
Graham Kendrick
Flowingly
Capo 4(C)
B (G)
E (C)
C♯m7 (Am7)
Such love, pure as the
F♯m7 (Dm7)
B7 (G)
F♯m7 (Dm7)
whit - est snow; Such love
B (G)
A/E (F/C)
E (C)
G♯sus (Esus)
weeps for the shame I know; Such
C♯m (Am)
C♯m/B (Am/G)
Amaj7 (Fmaj7)
A♯dim7 (F♯dim7)
love, pay-ing the debt I owe; O

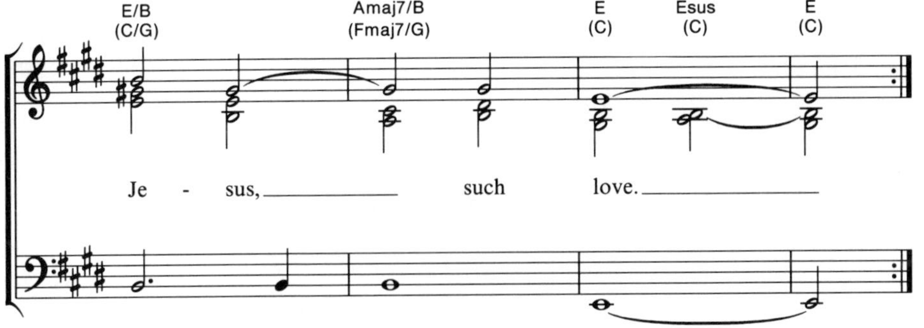
E/B
(C/G)
Amaj7/B
(Fmaj7/G)
E
(C)
Esus
(C)
E
(C)
Je - sus, such love.

1 Such love, pure as the whitest snow;
Such love weeps for the shame I know;
Such love, paying the debt I owe;
O Jesus, such love.

2 Such love, stilling my restlessness;
Such love, filling my emptiness;
Such love, showing me holiness;
O Jesus, such love.

3 Such love springs from eternity;
Such love, streaming through history;
Such love, fountain of life to me;
O Jesus, such love.

736 Spirit of God

Words and music
Chris Bowater

Broadly
Capo 2(C)
D (C) A/C♯ (G/B) Bm (Am) Bm/A (Am/G) G (F) D (C) D/A (C/G) A (G)
Spi - rit of God, show me Je-sus;
Em (Dm) F♯m/A (Em/G) A/G (G/F) F♯m7 (Em) Bm (Am) E9 (D9) C♯m/E (Bm/D) E7 (D7) Em7/A (Dm7/G) A7 (G7)
Re - move the dark - ness, let truth shine through.
D (C) A/C♯ (G/B) Bm (Am) Bm/A (Am/G) G (F) D (C) D/A (C/G) A (G)
Spi - rit of God, show me Je-sus;
Em (Dm) F♯m/A (Em/G) A/G (G/F) F♯m7 (Em) Bm (Am) Em7 (Dm) F♯m/A (Em/G) A7 (G7) D (C)
Re - veal the full - ness of His love to me!

Spirit of God, show me Jesus;
Remove the darkness, let truth shine through.
Spirit of God, show me Jesus;
Reveal the fullness of His love to me!

737 Spirit of the living God

Words and music
Paul Armstrong

C G/D C/E F F/G
Spi - rit of the liv - ing God fall a-fresh on me,
C G/B Am Am/G D/F♯ D G G7
Spi - rit of the liv - ing God fall a-fresh on me,
C C/E F A/E Dsus D/F♯ G G/F
Fill me a - new, fill me a - new,
E E/G♯ Am Dm7 C/G G C
Spi - rit of the Lord fall a - fresh on me.

Spirit of the living God fall afresh on me,
Spirit of the living God fall afresh on me,
Fill me anew, fill me anew,
Spirit of the Lord fall afresh on me.

738 Soften my heart

Words and music
Graham Kendrick

Prayerfully
Capo 2(C)
D (C)
Em (Dm)
Baug/E (Aaug/D)
Em7 (Dm7)
A (G) G/B (F/A) A/C♯ (G/B)
Soft - en my heart Lord, sof - ten my
D (C)
Dmaj7 (Cmaj7)
D6 (C6)
D (C)
Em (Dm)
heart; From all in - dif -
Baug/E (Aaug/D)
Em7 (Dm7)
A (G)
D (C)
F♯m/C♯ (Em/B)
Cdim (B♭dim)
- ference set me a - part To
Gmaj7 (Fmaj7)
A/G (G/F)
feel Your com - pas - sion, To weep with Your

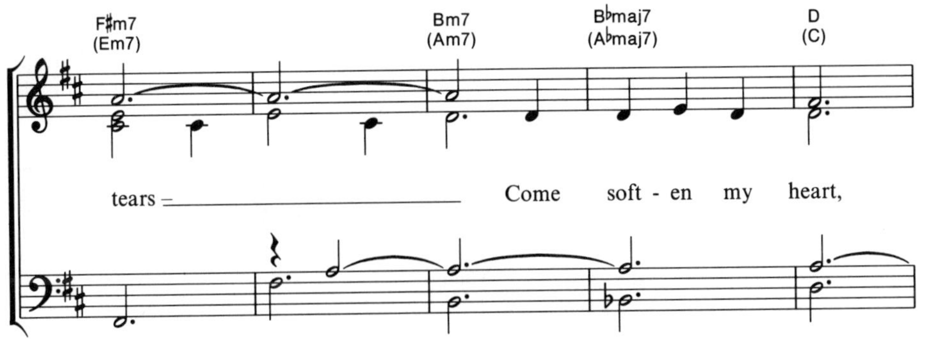
F♯m7
(Em7)
Bm7
(Am7)
B♭maj7
(A♭maj7)
D
(C)
tears –
Come soft - en my heart,

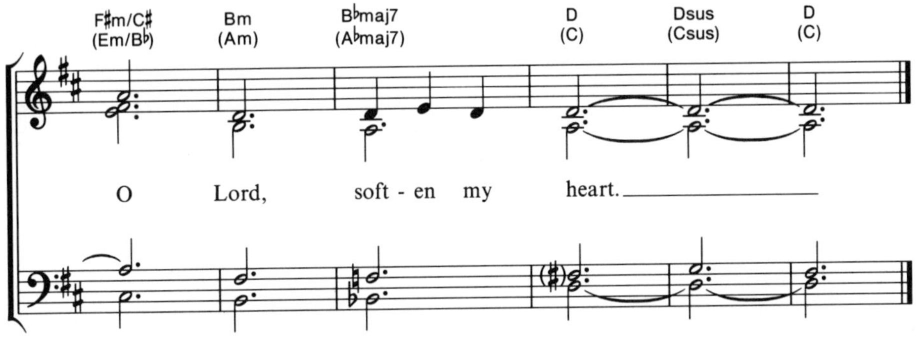
F♯m/C♯
(Em/B♭)
Bm
(Am)
B♭maj7
(A♭maj7)
D
(C)
Dsus
(Csus)
D
(C)
O Lord, soft - en my heart.

Soften my heart Lord, soften my heart;
From all indifference set me apart
To feel Your compassion,
To weep with Your tears –
Come soften my heart, O Lord, soften my heart.

739 Thank You for the cross

Words and music
Graham Kendrick

Capo 3(G)
B♭ (G)
E♭ (C)
B♭ (G)
Thank You for the cross, The price You paid for us, How You
Now our sins are gone, All for - giv - en, Cov-ered
Fm (Dm)
Cm7 (Am7)
B♭ (G)
E♭/B♭ (C/G)
B♭ (G)
gave Your - self So com - plete-ly, Pre - cious Lord. (Pre - cious Lord.)
by Your blood, All for - got - ten, Thank You Lord (Thank You Lord)
F7 (D7)
B♭ (G)
B♭/A (G/F♯)
Gm (Em)
Gm7/A (Em7/F♯)
Oh I love You Lord, Real - ly love You Lord. I will
B♭ (G)
Gm (Em)
C (A)
F7 (D7)
Cm7 (Am7)
ne-ver un-der-stand Why You love me. You're my deep-est joy, You're my

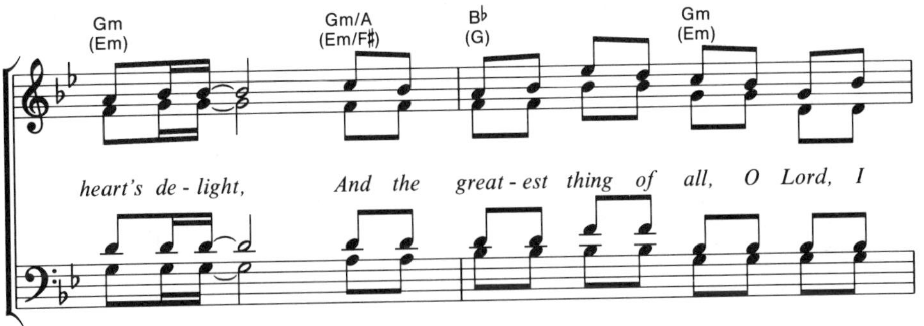
Gm
(Em)
Gm/A
(Em/F♯)
B♭
(G)
Gm
(Em)
heart's de - light, And the great - est thing of all, O Lord, I

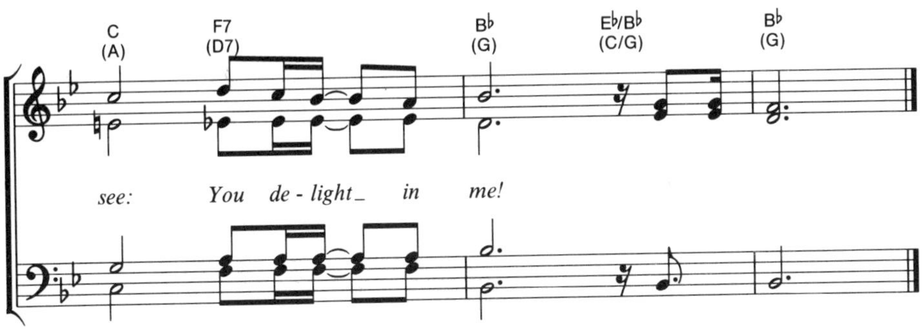
C
(A)
F7
(D7)
B♭
(G)
E♭/B♭
(C/G)
B♭
(G)
see: You de - light_ in me!

1 Thank You for the cross,
The price You paid for us,
How You gave Yourself
So completely,
Precious Lord. (Precious Lord.)
Now our sins are gone,
All forgiven,
Covered by Your blood,
All forgotten,
Thank You Lord (Thank You Lord)
Oh I love You Lord,
Really love You Lord.
I will never understand
Why You love me.
You're my deepest joy,
You're my heart's delight,
And the greatest thing of all,
O Lord, I see:
You delight in me!

2 For our healing there
Lord You suffered,
And to take our fear
You poured out Your love,
Precious Lord. (Precious Lord.)
Calvary's work is done,
You have conquered,
Able now to save
So completely,
Thank You Lord. (Thank You Lord.)
Oh I love You . . .

740 Take heart and praise our God

Christchurch

Words: David Mowbray
Music: C Steggall (1826–1905)

C G/B Am Dm G C F C/E Am7/D G7 C
Take heart and praise our God; Re - joice and clap your hands – His

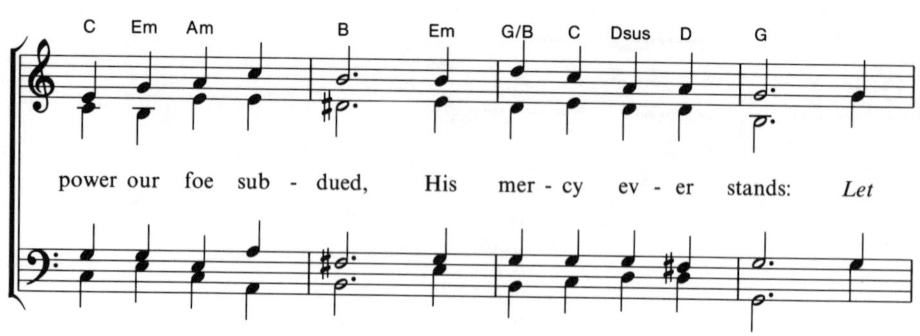
C Em Am B Em G/B C Dsus D G
power our foe sub - dued, His mer - cy ev - er stands: Let

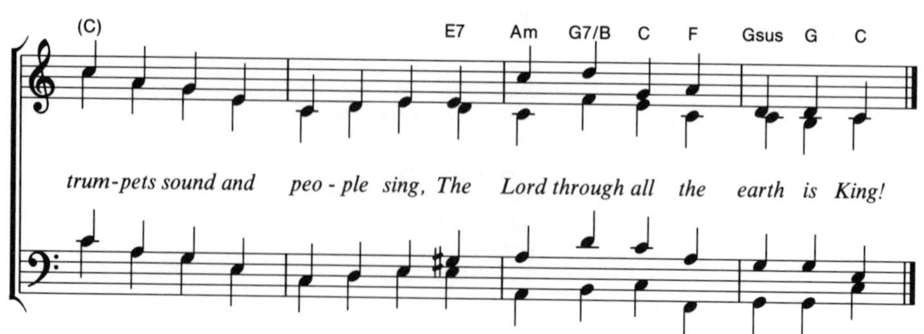
(C) E7 Am G7/B C F Gsus G C
trum-pets sound and peo - ple sing, The Lord through all the earth is King!

1 Take heart and praise our God;
Rejoice and clap your hands –
His power our foe subdued,
His mercy ever stands:
Let trumpets sound and people sing,
The Lord through all the earth is King!

2 Take heart, but sing with fear,
Exalt His worthy name;
With mind alert and clear
Now celebrate His fame:
Let trumpets sound . . .

3 Take heart for future days,
For tasks as yet unknown –
The God whose name we praise
Is seated on the throne:
Let trumpets sound . . .

4 Take heart and trust in God
The Father and the Son –
God is our strength and shield,
His Spirit guides us on:
Let trumpets sound . . .

741 The Lord has led forth

Words and music
Chris Bowater
Music arranged Phil Burt

D Em7 D/F♯ G D/F♯ Em7
The Lord has led forth His peo - ple with joy,
D/F♯ Em7 D Em7 D/F♯ A D/A G/A A7
And His cho-sen ones with sing - ing, sing - ing; The
D Em7 D/F♯ G D/F♯ Em7 D/F♯ Em7
Lord has led forth His peo - ple with joy, And His
D Em7 D/F♯ A7 D G D
Fine
cho - sen ones with sing - ing.

Bm
F♯m
He has given to them the lands of the na-
Bm
F♯m
G
D/F♯
-tions, To pos-sess the fruit and keep His laws, And praise,
Em7
G/A
A7
D.𝄋 al Fine
praise His name.
The

The Lord has led forth His people with joy,
And His chosen ones with singing, singing;
The Lord has led forth His people with joy,
And His chosen ones with singing.
He has given to them the lands of the nations,
To possess the fruit and keep His laws,
And praise, praise His name.
The Lord has led forth His people with joy,
And His chosen ones with singing, singing;
The Lord has led forth His people with joy,
And His chosen ones with singing.

742 The Lord is King

Words and music
Graham Kendrick

Triumphantly
Capo 4(C)
E (C) Asus2 (G) A (F) E (C)
The Lord is King, He is migh - ty in bat - tle,
A (F) E (C) C♯m (Am) F♯m (Dm)
Work-ing won-ders, Glor-ious in ma - jes -
F♯m/B (G) E/B (G) A/B (G) B7 (G7) E (C) Asus2 (G) A (F) E (C)
- ty. The Lord is King – So ma - jes - tic in pow - er!
A (F) E (C) C♯m (Am) F♯m (Dm) B7 (G7)
His right hand Has shat-tered the en - e - my.

E
(C)
G♯m7
(Em7)
F♯m7
(Dm7)
B
(G)
E
(C)
G♯m7
(Em7)
This is my God
And I will praise Him;
This is my God
F♯m7
(Dm7)
B
(G)
E
(C)
G♯m7
(Em7)
F♯m7
(Dm7)
B
(G)
My strength and song
And my sal - va -
And I will praise Him:
E
(C)
G♯m7
(Em7)
F♯m7
(Dm7)
A
(F)
B7
(G7)
E
(C)
- tion,
And my sal - va - tion,
My strength and song
And my sal - va - tion.

743 This Child

Words and music
Graham Kendrick

Calypso
D
G6
A7
D
This
G6
A7
Child, se-cret-ly comes in the night, Oh, this Child, hid-ing a hea-
D
G6
-ven - ly light, Oh, this Child, com-ing to us___ like a stran-ger,
A7
D
G
This hea - ven-ly Child. *This Child, hea-ven come down*

D
A7
D
_ now to be with us here, Hea-ven-ly love_ and mer - cy ap -
G
D
Asus
A
- pear, Soft-ly in awe_ and won-der come near To this hea-ven-ly
1.2.
3.
D.𝄋
4.
Child.
2 This Child.
3 This
This Child.

1 This Child, secretly comes in the night,
Oh, this Child, hiding a heavenly light,
Oh, this Child, coming to us like a stranger,
This heavenly Child.
This Child, heaven come down now to be with us here,
Heavenly love and mercy appear,
Softly in awe and wonder come near
To this heavenly Child.

2 This Child, rising on us like the sun,
Oh this Child, given to light everyone,
Oh this Child, guiding our feet on the pathway
To peace on earth.
This Child, heaven come down . . .

3 This Child, raising the humble and poor,
Oh this Child, making the proud ones to fall;
This Child, filling the hungry with good things,
This heavenly Child.
This Child, heaven come down . . .

744 There is a fountain

St. Mary

Words: William Cowper (1731–1800)
Music: from Prys' *Psalter* 1621

Capo 5(Am)
Dm (Am) Am (Em) B♭ (F) F (C) Gm (Dm) D (A) F (D)
There is a foun - tain filled with blood Drawn
C (G) Dm (Am) C (G) F (C) C (G) G (D) C (G) F (C)
from Em - man - uel's veins; And sin - ners, plunged be -
C (G) G (D) C (G) F (D) B♭ (F) Dm (Am) A7 (E7) Dm (Am)
- neath that flood, Lose all their guil - ty stains.

1 There is a fountain filled with blood
Drawn from Emmanuel's veins;
And sinners, plunged beneath that flood,
Lose all their guilty stains.

2 The dying thief rejoiced to see
That fountain in his day;
And there may I, as vile as he,
Wash all my sins away.

3 Dear dying Lamb! Your precious blood
Shall never lose its power,
Till all the ransomed Church of God
Be saved, to sin no more.

4 E'er since, by faith, I saw the stream
Your flowing wounds supply,
Redeeming love has been my theme,
And shall be till I die.

5 Then in a nobler, sweeter song,
I'll sing Your power to save,
When this poor lisping, stammering tongue
Lies silent in the grave.

745 Tonight

(Glory to God)

Words and music
Graham Kendrick

G/B C
G/C C
G/C C Csus
1 To-night, while all the world was
(2 A-fraid) we cov - ered up our
G/A Am
G/B C
G/C C
sleep - ing, A light ex-plo -
fa - ces, A-mazed at what
G/C C
Gsus
G/B C
- ded in the skies. And then,
our ears did hear. Good news
G/C C G/C C Csus G/A Am
G/B C
as glo - ry did sur - round us, A voice,
of joy for all the peo - ple To-day

G/C C G/C C Gsus G
an an - gel did ap - pear!
a Sav - iour has ap - peared!
C G/C C F/C C G/C C
WOMEN: Glo - ry to God
MEN: Glo - ry to God in the
F/C C G/B Am
in the high - est, ALL: Be
high - est, And on the earth,
D G C G/C C
peace from heaven! MEN: Glo - ry to

F/C C G/C C F/C C
WOMEN: Glo - ry to God in the
God in the high - est,
G/B Am Dm7 G7
high - est, ALL: Be peace from
And on the earth,
C Csus C C Csus
heaven!
1. 2.
C G/B C C Am
2 A-fraid And so to Beth - le - hem

Fmaj
Am
To find it all was
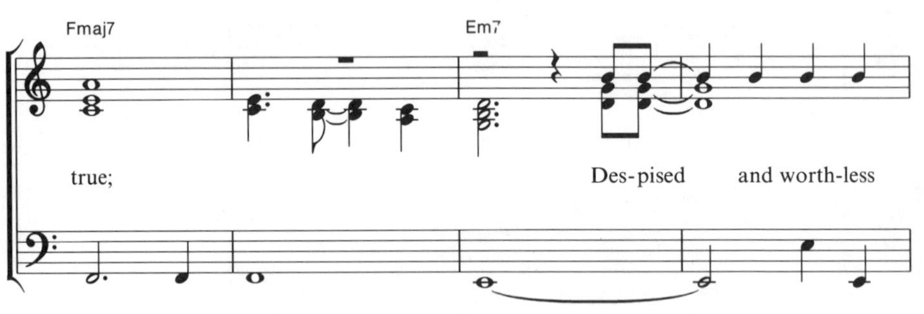
Fmaj7
Em7
true;
Des-pised and worth-less

Fmaj7
Dm
shep - herds,
We were the first to

Gsus
G
Gsus
G
know!
f

C G/C C F/C C G/C C
WOMEN: Glo - ry to God
MEN: Glo - ry to God in the
F/C C G/B Am
in the high - est, ALL: Be
high - est, And on the earth,
1.3.
D G
peace from heaven!
2.
Dm7 G7 C
peace from heaven!
4.
Dm7 G7 C Csus C Csus C Csus C
peace from heaven!

746 The Spirit of the Lord

Words and music
Chris Bowater
With strength
G F/G C
1 The Spi - rit of the
2 And He has called on
3 Let right-eous-ness a -
G G/B Am G/D D7
Lord, The sove - reign Lord, is on me
me To bind up all the bro - ken hearts,
- rise And blos - som as a gar - den;
C G Bm7 Am7
Be-cause He has a - noin - ted me To preach good news
To mi - ni-ster re - lease to ev - ery Cap - ti - va - ted
Let praise be-gin to spring in ev - ery Tongue and
D7 C/D D7 G Bm7
to the poor:
soul:
na - tion:
Pro-claim-ing Je - -

Am7
D7
G
Bm7
Am7
D7
G
Em
- sus, on-ly Je - - - sus – It is Je - sus, Sav-iour,
Am
D7
G
Em7
Am
D7
Heal-er and Bap-tiz-er, And the Migh - ty King, the Vic-tor and De-liv-erer – He is
C
G/B
Am7
Am7/D
G
Lord, He is Lord, He is Lord.

1 The Spirit of the Lord,
The sovereign Lord, is on me
Because He has anointed me
To preach good news to the poor:
Proclaiming Jesus, only Jesus –
It is Jesus, Saviour, Healer and Baptizer,
And the Mighty King, the Victor and Deliverer –
He is Lord, He is Lord, He is Lord.

2 And He has called on me
To bind up all the broken hearts,
To minister release to every
Captivated soul:
Proclaiming Jesus . . .

3 Let righteousness arise
And blossom as a garden;
Let praise begin to spring in every
Tongue and nation:
Proclaiming Jesus . . .

747 The earth was dark

(Lights to the world)

Words and music
John Daniels and
Phil Thompson

Spirited
Capo 5(Am)
Dm (Am) C (G) B♭ (F) F/A (C/E) B♭ (F) C (G) Dm (Am) C/E (G/B) F (C)
The earth was dark un - til You spoke – Then all was light and
C (G) C/E (G/B) F (C) Dm (Am) C (G) B♭ (F) F/A (C/E) B♭ (F) C (G) Dm (Am)
all was peace; Yet still, O God, so ma - ny wait
C/E (G/B) F (C) G (D) C (G)
To see the flame of love re - leased.
Am (Em) Dm7 (Am7) Gm7 (Am7) C (G) Am7 (Em7) Dm7 (Am7)
Lights to the world! O Light di - vine, Kin - dle in us a

Gm7
(Am7)
C
(G)
A/C♯
(E/G♯)
Dm
(Am)
C/E
(G/B)
Cm/F
(Gm/C)
B♭
(F)
F/A
(C/E)
migh-ty flame, Till ev-ery heart, con-sumed by love Shall rise to
Gm
(Dm)
C7
(G7)
F
(C)
F/A
(C/E)
1.2.3.
Gm7
(Dm7)
C7sus C7
(G7sus)(G7)
4.
F
(C)
praise Your ho - ly Name!

1 The earth was dark until You spoke –
Then all was light and all was peace;
Yet still, O God, so many wait
To see the flame of love released.
Lights to the world! O Light divine,
Kindle in us a mighty flame,
Till every heart, consumed by love
Shall rise to praise Your holy Name!

2 In Christ You gave Your gift of life
To save us from the depth of the night:
O come and set our spirits free
And draw us to Your perfect light.
Lights to the world . . .

3 Where there is fear may we bring joy
And healing to a world in pain:
Lord, build Your kingdom through our lives
Till Jesus walks this earth again.
Lights to the world . . .

4 O burn in us, that we may burn
With love that triumphs in despair;
And touch our lives with such a fire
That souls may search and find You there.
Lights to the world . . .

748 The earth is the Lord's

Words and music
Graham Kendrick

With strength
D G D
MEN: The earth is the Lord's
WOMEN: And ev - ery - thing in it.
MEN: The
Em A
earth is the Lord's
WOMEN: The work of His hands.
MEN: The earth is the
G D G
Lord's
WOMEN: And ev - ery - thing in it.
ALL And all things were
3rd time to Coda
D A7 D Dsus D
made for His glo - ry!

A7
D
Bm
Em
The moun-tains are His, The seas and the
A7
D
Bm
Em
is - lands, The ci - ties and towns, The hou - ses and
A
D
Bm
Em
streets: Let re - bels bow down And wor - ship be -
A7
G
D
A7
- fore Him, For all things were made for His glo -
D
Dsus
D
A7
repeat twice
- ry! The

CODA
A7
D
G
D
MEN: The earth is the Lord's
WOMEN: And ev - ery-thing in it.
MEN: The
Em
A
earth is the Lord's
WOMEN: The work of His hands.
MEN: The earth is the
G
D
G
Lord's
WOMEN: And ev - ery - thing in it.
ALL And all things were
D
G
D
G
made, Yes, all things were made, And all things were
D
A7
D
made for His glo - ry!

749 What a mighty God we serve

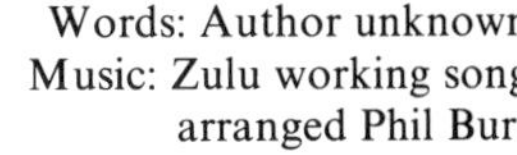
Words: Author unknown
Music: Zulu working song
arranged Phil Burt

With strength and joy

G/D D7 G C G C G D7

What a migh - ty God we serve, What a

G D7 G G7

migh - ty God we serve, What a migh - ty God we serve,

C D7 G Am D7 G C G

What a migh - ty God we serve.

1 What a mighty God we serve . . .

2 He created you and me . . .

3 He has all the power to save . . .

4 Let us praise the living God . . .

5 What a mighty God we serve . . .

750 We break this bread

Words and music
Chris Rolinson

Thoughtfully
Capo 1(D)
A♭/B♭ (G/A)
E♭ (D)
E♭maj7 (Dmaj7)
MEN: We break this bread to share in the
A♭maj7 (Gmaj7)
A♭6 (G6)
B♭ (A)
A♭/B♭ (G/A)
bo - dy of Christ: WOMEN: We break this
E♭ (D)
E♭maj7 (Dmaj7)
A♭maj7 (Gmaj7)
A♭6 (G6)
bread to share in the bo - dy of
B6 (A)
Gm/B♭ (F♯m/A)
A♭ (G)
B♭/A♭ (A/G)
Christ: ALL: Though we are ma - ny, We are one

Gm
(F♯m)
Cm7
(Bm7)
Fm7
(Em7)
bo - dy, Be-cause we all share We
1.
A♭/B♭ B♭7 A♭/B♭ B♭7 E♭maj7
(G/A) (A7) (G/A) (A7) (Dmaj7)
E♭7
(D7)
3
all share in one bread. Though we are
2.
A♭/B♭ B♭7 A♭/B♭ B♭7 A♭/E♭
(G/A) (A7) (G/A) (A7) (G/D)
E♭
(D)
all share in one bread.

1 MEN We break this bread to share in the body of Christ:
WOMEN We break this bread to share in the body of Christ:
ALL Though we are many,
We are one body,
Because we all share
We all share in one bread.

2 MEN We drink this cup to share in the body of Christ:
WOMEN We drink this cup to share in the body of Christ:
ALL Though we are many,
We are one body,
Because we all share
We all share in one cup.

751 We shall stand

Words and music
Graham Kendrick

Rocky
Capo 3(D)
Fsus2
(Dsus2)
Dm
(Bm)
We shall stand, with our feet on the Rock;
Bb
(G)
Bb/C
(G/A)
What-ev-er men may say, we'll lift Your name up high
Bb/C
(G/A)
Fsus2
(Dsus2)
Dm
(Bm)
And we shall walk through the dark - est night;
last time to Coda
F/Bb
(D/G)
Bb
(G)
Bb/C
(G/A)
Fsus2
(Dsus2)
Set-ting our fa - ces like flint, We'll walk in-to the light!

F
(D)
F/A
(D/F♯)
B♭maj7
(Gmaj7)
C/F
(A/D)
F
(D)
1 Lord, You have cho - sen me for fruit-ful-ness,
2 Lord, as Your wit - nes-ses You've ap-point-ed us,
F/A
(D/F♯)
B♭maj7
(Gmaj7)
F
(D)
To be trans-formed in-to Your like -
And with Your Ho - ly Spi-rit a - noint - ed
C
(A)
Dm
(Bm)
B♭
(G)
Csus
(Asus)
- ness: I'm going to
us: And so I'll
fight on through till I see You Face
C
(A)
to face.
CODA
F
(D)

752 We Your people

Words and music
Adrian Snell

Moderato
C Dm/C Am C/E Am7 Dm7 Dm/C
1 We Your peo - ple bow be - fore_ You Bro - ken and a -
3 Fa - ther, in this hour of dan - ger We will turn to
G/B Gsus G7 F/A G7/B C2 Fmaj7 G/F
- shamed; We have turned on Your cre - a - tion
You: O for - give us, Lord, for - give us
C/E Dm7 F/G G7 C Am7 F/A Em/G G
Crushed the life You free - ly_ gave.
And our lives and faith re - new.
C F/A Gsus G C Dm/C Am C/E Am7
2 Lord, have mer - cy on Your child - ren
4 Pour Your Ho - ly Spi - rit on_ us,

Dm7
Dm/C
G/B
A/C♯
Dm7
Em7
Weep - ing and in fear:
Set our hearts a - flame:
For You_ are our
All shall_ see Your
Fmaj7 Em7
Dm7
C/E
Dm/F
1.
G7
C
God and_ Sav-iour - Fa - ther_ in Your love draw near.
power in the na-tions - May we bring glo - ry
Am7 F/A Em/G G
C
F/A
G7
2.
G7
to Your
Am
Dm7
C/E
Dm/F
C/G
G7
C
name, may we bring glo - ry to Your name!

1 We Your people bow before You
Broken and ashamed;
We have turned on Your creation
Crushed the life You freely gave.

2 Lord, have mercy on Your children
Weeping and in fear:
For You are our God and Saviour
Father in Your love draw near.

3 Father, in this hour of danger
We will turn to You:
O forgive us, Lord, forgive us
And our lives and faith renew.

4 Pour Your Holy Spirit on us,
Set our hearts aflame:
All shall see Your power in the nations
May we bring glory to Your name.

753 What kind of love is this

Words and music
Bryn and Sally Haworth

Moderato
C G C G7
What kind of love is this,
kind of love is this?
C C G7 C
That gave it-self for me?
A love I've ne-ver known.
F G
I am the
I did-n't e-ven
1.
C G/B Am D7
v.2
guil-ty one, Yet I

G7
go
free.
What
2.
Am
F
C
know
His
name,
what
kind
of
love
G
C
F/C
1.2.
C
D.%
3.
is
this?
What

1 What kind of love is this,
That gave itself for me?
I am the guilty one,
Yet I go free.
What kind of love is this?
A love I've never known.
I didn't even know His Name,
What kind of love is this?

2 What kind of man is this,
That died in agony?
He who had done no wrong
Was crucified for me.
What kind of man is this,
Who laid aside His throne
That I may know the love of God?
What kind of man is this?

3 By grace I have been saved,
It is the gift of God.
He destined me to be His son,
Such is His love.
No eye has ever seen,
No ear has ever heard,
Nor has the heart of man conceived,
What kind of love is this?

754 Who can sound

Words and music
Graham Kendrick
With feeling
Capo 1(A)
G♭ (F) Cdim/E♭ (Bdim) G♭/B♭ (F) B♭ (A) Cm7 (Bm7) Cm7/F F (E)
1 Who can
B♭ (A) F/B♭ (E) E♭/B♭ (D) B♭ (A) Gm (F♯m) Gm/F E♭ (D)
sound the depths of sor-row In the Fa - ther heart of God, For the
(2) scorned the truth You gave us, We have bowed to o - ther lords, We have
MEN: (3) stand be - fore Your an-ger; Who can face Your pier-cing eyes? For You
F/E♭ (E) B♭/D (A) Gm7 (F♯m7) C9 (B) Cm7 (Bm7) F (E)
child-ren we've re - jec - ted, For the lives so deep - ly scarred? And each
sac - ri - ficed the child-ren On the alt - ars of our gods. O let
love the weak and help-less, And You hear the vic-tims' cries. ALL: Yes, You
B♭ (A) F/B♭ (E) E♭/B♭ (D) B♭ (A) Gm (F♯m) Gm/F E♭ (D)
light that we've ex - tin-guished Has bought dark - ness to our land:
truth a - gain shine on us, Let Your ho - ly fear de - scend:
are a God of jus - tice, And Your judge-ment sure-ly comes:

C♯dim
(Cdim)
B♭
(A)
G♭
(F)
B♭
(A)
Up - on the na - tion, up - on the na - tion Have
Up - on the na - tion, up - on the na - tion Have
Up - on the na - tion, up - on the na - tion Have
1-4.
5.
Fsus
(Esus)
F
(E)
B♭
(A)
F/B♭
(E)
E♭/B♭
(D)
E♭m/B♭
(Dm)
B♭
(A)
mer - cy Lord! 2 We have Lord!
mer - cy Lord! MEN: 3 Who can
mer - cy Lord!

1 Who can sound the depths of sorrow
In the Father heart of God,
For the children we've rejected,
For the lives so deeply scarred?
And each light that we've extinguished
Has bought darkness to our land:
Upon the nation, upon the nation
Have mercy Lord!

2 We have scorned the truth You gave us,
We have bowed to other lords,
We have sacrificed the children
On the altars of our gods.
O let truth again shine on us,
Let Your holy fear descend:
Upon the nation, upon the nation
Have mercy Lord!

MEN
3 Who can stand before Your anger;
Who can face Your piercing eyes?
For You love the weak and helpless,
And You hear the victims' cries.
ALL
Yes, You are a God of justice,
And Your judgement surely comes:
Upon the nation, upon the nation
Have mercy Lord!

WOMEN
4 Who will stand against the violence?
Who will comfort those who mourn?
In an age of cruel rejection,
Who will build for love a home?
ALL
Come and shake us into action,
Come and melt our hearts of stone:
Upon Your people, upon Your people,
Have mercy Lord!

5 Who can sound the depths of mercy
In the Father heart of God?
For there is a Man of sorrows
Who for sinners shed His blood.
He can heal the wounds of nations,
He can wash the guilty clean:
Because of Jesus, because of Jesus,
Have mercy Lord!

755 With all my heart

Words and music
Paul Field

Steadily
G D/F♯ C/E D G D/F♯ C D
With
G D/F♯ Csus2/E D G D/F♯ C/E D
all my heart I thank You Lord. With
G D/F♯ Csus2/E D G D/F♯ C/E D
all my heart I thank You Lord, For this
Em D Csus2 D G/B Am7 G D/F♯ C D
bread and wine we break, For this sac - ra - ment we take, For the for -

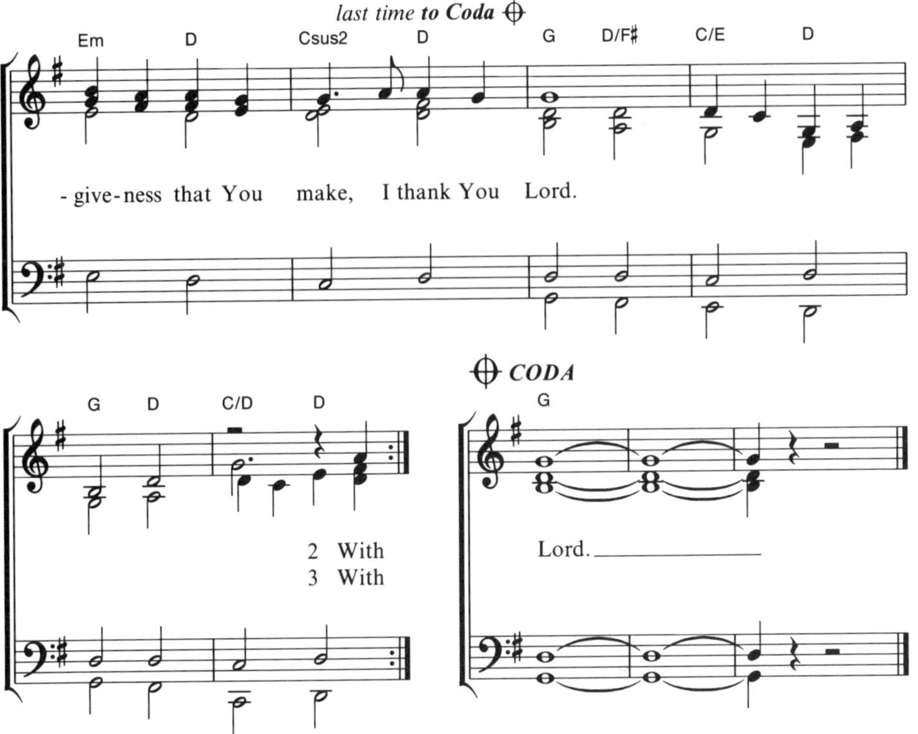
last time to Coda
Em
D
Csus2
D
G
D/F♯
C/E
D
- give-ness that You make, I thank You Lord.
CODA
G
D
C/D
D
2 With
3 With
G
Lord.

1 With all my heart I thank You Lord.
With all my heart I thank You Lord,
For this bread and wine we break,
For this sacrament we take,
For the forgiveness that You make,
I thank You Lord.

2 With all my soul I thank You Lord.
With all my soul I thank You Lord,
For this victory that You've won,
For this taste of things to come,
For this love that makes us one,
I thank You Lord.

3 With all my voice I thank You Lord.
With all my voice I thank You Lord,
For the sacrifice of pain,
For the Spirit and the flame,
For the power of Your Name,
I thank You Lord.

756 Wonderful Counsellor, Jesus

Words and music
Bill Yarger

Tenderly
C/G C G/A Am7
C/D Dm F/G G C/G C
1 Won-der-ful
2 Migh-ty God,
3 Ev - er - last - ing
4 Prince of peace,
5 Won-der-ful
G/A Am7 C/D Dm7 F/G
Coun-sel-lor Je - sus:
Son of God, Je - sus;
Fa - ther, Je - sus;
rule my heart, Je - sus;
Coun-sel-lor Je - sus;
C/D Dm7 C/G Dm7 Dm/C C
Search me, know me, Je - sus;
Name a-bove all o-ther names, Je - sus:
Ho-ly and un - change-a-ble, Je - sus:
Know my ev - ery an-xious thought, Je - sus;
Migh-ty God, Son of God, Je - sus;

Gm7
Gm7/C
C7
G/A
Am
G
Am
Lead_ me, ___ guide_ me,_
Glo - ri - fy, ___ mag - ni - fy,_
Fill me with Your pre - sence,
Calm my fears, ___ dry my tears,
Ev - er - last - ing Fa - ther,
Fmaj7
F
Dm7
F/G
G7
G/C
C
Je - sus ___ Won-der-ful ___
Je - sus ___ Migh-ty God, ___
Je - sus ___ Ev - er - last - ing
Je - sus ___ Prince of peace, ___
Je - sus ___ Prince of peace, ___
1-4.
5.
C/D
Dm7
F/C
C
G/C
C
Coun-sel-lor_ Je - sus._
Son of God, Je - sus._
Fa - ther, Je - sus._
rule my heart, Je - sus._
rule my heart, Je - sus!_

1 Wonderful Counsellor Jesus:
Search me, know me, Jesus;
Lead me, guide me, Jesus –
Wonderful Counsellor Jesus.

2 Mighty God, Son of God, Jesus;
Name above all other names, Jesus:
Glorify, magnify, Jesus –
Mighty God, Son of God, Jesus.

3 Everlasting Father, Jesus;
Holy and unchangeable, Jesus:
Fill me with Your presence, Jesus –
Everlasting Father, Jesus.

4 Prince of peace, rule my heart, Jesus;
Know my every anxious thought, Jesus;
Calm my fears, dry my tears, Jesus –
Prince of peace, rule my heart, Jesus.

5 Wonderful Counsellor Jesus;
Mighty God, Son of God, Jesus;
Everlasting Father, Jesus –
Prince of peace, rule my heart, Jesus.

757 When peace like a river

Words: Horatio G Spafford
Music: Philip P Bliss
arranged Phil Burt

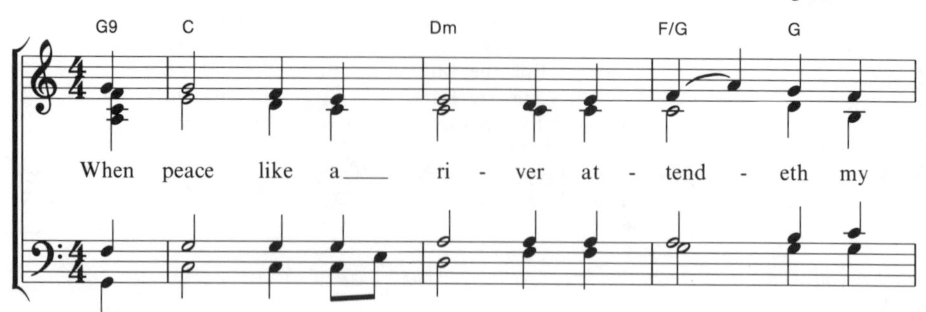
G9 C Dm F/G G
When peace like a___ ri - ver at - tend - eth my

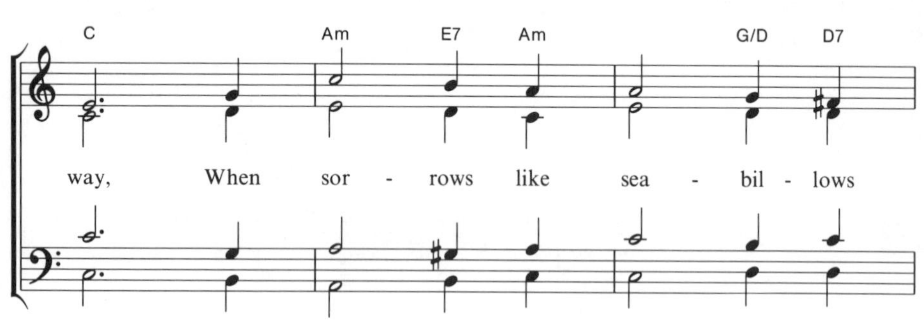
C Am E7 Am G/D D7
way, When sor - rows like sea - bil - lows

G G7 C
roll;___ What - ev - er my

F A7 Dm D7 G C Dm
lot You have taught me to say, 'It is___ well, it is

C/G
G
C
F/C
C
well with my soul.' ______ It is
(well with my soul)
G
C
well, ______ with my soul. ______ It is
(it is well)
(with my soul)
F
C/G
G
C
F
C
well, it is well with my soul. ______

1 When peace like a river attendeth my way,
When sorrows like sea-billows roll;
Whatever my lot You have taught me to say,
'It is well, it is well with my soul.'

2 Though Satan should buffet, if trials should come,
Let this blessed assurance control,
That Christ has regarded my helpless estate,
And has shed His own blood for my soul.

3 My sin – O the bliss of this glorious thought –
My sin – not in part – but the whole
Is nailed to His Cross; and I bear it no more;
Praise the Lord, praise the Lord, O my soul.

4 For me, be it Christ, be it Christ hence to live!
If Jordan above me shall roll.
No pang shall be mine, for in death as in life
You will whisper Your peace to my soul.

5 But Lord, it's for You for Your coming we wait,
The sky, not the grave, is our goal:
O, trump of the angel! O voice of the Lord!
Blessed hope! blessed rest of my soul.

758 You are beautiful

Words and music
Mark Altrogge

Majestically
Capo 2(G)
A (G)
E/A (D/G)
Dsus2/A (C/G)
You are beau-ti-ful be-yond de-scrip - tion,_ Too mar-vel-lous for words,
A (G)
E/A (D/G)
_ Too won-der-ful for com - pre-hen - sion,___ Like
Dsus2/A (C/G)
E (D)
C# (B)
F#m7 (Em7)
no-thing ev-er seen or heard. Who can grasp Your in-fi-nite wis-
B9 (A9)
D (C)
E (D)
-dom? Who can fa-thom the depth of Your love?_ You are

A
(G)
E/A
(D/G)
D
(C)
Esus
(Dsus)
beau-ti-ful be-yond de-scrip - tion, Ma-jes-ty,___ en-throned a - bove.
A
(G)
Esus
(Dsus)
E
(D)
A
(G)
E/A
(D/G)
Dsus2/A
(C/G)
___ And I stand, I stand in awe of You.___ I
A
(G)
E/A
(D/G)
Dsus2/A
(C/G)
G♯7sus
(F♯sus)
C♯7
(B7)
stand, I stand in awe of You.___ Ho-ly God, to whom all
Dmaj
(Cmaj7)
D♯m7(♭5)
(C♯dim)
Bm7
(Am7)
E
(D)
D/A
(C/G)
A
(G)
praise is due, I stand in awe of You.

You are beautiful beyond description,
Too marvellous for words,
Too wonderful for comprehension,
Like nothing ever seen or heard.
Who can grasp Your infinite wisdom?
Who can fathom the depth of Your love?
You are beautiful beyond description,
Majesty, enthron'd above.
And I stand, I stand in awe of You.
I stand, I stand in awe of You.
Holy God, to whom all praise is due,
I stand in awe of You.

Index of First Lines

Titles which differ from first lines are shown in italics